PURPLE ON THE INSIDE

PURPLE ON THE INSIDE

How J.B. Hunt Transport Set Itself Apart
in a Field Full of Brown Cows

Kirk Thompson and Matthew A. Waller

FAYETTEVILLE

2019

Dedicated to J.B. Hunt Transport Services employees, past and present, who are responsible for JBHT being purple on the inside. And to future team members, who will continue to paint with the purple brush.

—KIRK THOMPSON

Dedicated to the faculty, staff, students, and alumni of the Sam M. Walton College of Business, who are responsible for our EPIC values—excellence, professionalism, innovation, and collegiality.

—MATTHEW WALLER

CONTENTS

An Innovative Difference

E very so often, you encounter someone you know will make a difference in the world. You might not be sure how or when—you just know it. For me, Kirk Thompson was just such a person.

Kirk and I met in 1988 when I was a young transportation analyst and he was president and CEO of J.B. Hunt Transport Service. I was immediately struck by Kirk's intense focus on what his company needed to do over the next five and ten years, rather than on its stellar recent record. He spoke with passion about JBHT's culture—a passion for not only being the best, but for developing long-term businesses that others could not replicate and customers could not do without. From the beginning, I was fired up. Kirk had this fantastic maxim: "At JBHT, we tolerate innovation." Little did I know, that would become the seed of the purple cow pasture JBHT has cultivated today.

Throughout this remarkable book, you will find references to the purple cow, the core of JBHT's culture and way of thinking. It has much to do with essential products and services that others cannot replicate. Traditional brown cows are a commodity you see in fields all over the country. Purple cows are one of a kind—and that in a nutshell embodies JBHT. All along, the successes of its past did not matter unless it was a step ahead of the present. Several purple cows and $12 billion of equity market value later, that guiding principle has clearly worked.

Purple on the Inside portrays the transformation of a company within a very basic industry—trucking—into a logistics powerhouse that provides virtually all facets of freight transportation within the United States. For investors, students, business executives, and academics, the book serves as a first-rate study of how to succeed in business. JBHT began without a consultant's playbook in hand, but it recognized several key tenets that any business theorist would stand behind: barriers to entry are essential, the value proposition must be best for customers and garner strong returns on capital for shareholders, and investments in information technology are a necessity rather than a luxury. And those are only a few of them. Perhaps most importantly, JBHT has constantly tolerated innovation, which has driven culture, growth, and superior financial returns.

Kirk and his co-author, Matthew Waller, are the ideal narrators to bring you this singular success story. Kirk continues to live it as the company's chairman and has been central to all its strategic decisions, good and bad, for more than four decades. He has brought a zeal to the company that I rarely see in other executives. As both a Wall Street analyst and institutional investor, I have known him for thirty years. I have always admired how consistently he would restate his credos: *we must do things differently, offer a better service that others cannot replicate, and earn in excess of our cost of capital.* To the outside public, his unceasing fervor for the company was clear in the way he challenged people with respect rather than arrogance. At investor conferences, Kirk would post slides illustrating JBHT's financial returns and valuation, and ask the hard question: "Why are you paying less for JBHT despite the company having higher returns?" No one else did that. He's always been spot on. I love that about him.

Co-author Matthew Waller, dean of the Sam M. Walton College of Business at the University of Arkansas, has been a leader in academia and logistics for many years and has authored several books and articles on supply chain and inventory management. He has worked with the company on many logistics-related projects, giving him a unique vantage from which to observe JBHT's growth. Together, our co-authors bring practical and academic perspectives to a story of hard-fought ascent.

At one time or another, we all get the speech that the proof is in the pudding and the numbers don't lie. Well, I am a big believer in such tried-and-true sayings. So here goes: 8,094. That's the percent increase in JBHT's stock from IPO date in 1983 to the present. That represents basically two to three times the performance of industry household names such as Federal Express and Union Pacific and roughly five times that of the S&P 500 index. Not bad for a trucker whose sales at IPO were $63 million and equity valuation exceeded $200 million. Heck, that increase would be pretty good for a tech company from Silicon Valley. Moreover, JBHT did it organically. Practically all of its sales are from homegrown lines of business, virtually unheard of these days.

So how did a small company evolve into a nationwide logistics provider with a current equity value of just more than $14 billion?

The change began in the early 1980s, the period just after deregulation of the trucking industry. Some companies sold off their trucking arms or went out of business, unable to handle the newly created competitive landscape. Others got bigger and more profitable. JBHT stood at the head of the pack. Earnings per share rose from $0.64 in 1984 to $1.40 in 1988. The stock appreciated more than 175 percent, roughly twice the performance of the S&P 500 (and almost three times the Dow Jones Transportation Index). Life was good.

By the late 1980s, however, Kirk and his team sensed trouble brewing. The company was starting to look brown. JBHT flirted with doing what everyone else did. And as more companies received funding from Wall Street and entered the market, the pasture was becoming overcrowded.

The team chose to embrace the changing winds. The crucial transformation, Quantum, was unveiled to the outside world on December 13, 1989. On that day, the way freight moved across America was altered forever—and Purple Cow No. 1 was born. I am not going to give too much of the excitement away. Suffice it to say that while Quantum checks the boxes of many important business theories, it was born out of plain old common sense. The JBHT intermodal alliance with the railroad industry would bring shippers a far cheaper service while promising nearly comparable transit times and less pollution. Be Purple: Do the unthinkable. A strategic alliance with the enemy: A railroad. Everyone in the industry said, "This is not done." JBHT management said, "Why not?" The rest is history.

Over the following decades, other purple cows emerged, all born out of JBHT's intense desire to offer specialized services and to do what others wouldn't or couldn't. Two of them—Dedicated Contract Services (DCS) and Integrated Capacity Solutions (ICS)—have thrived in the JBHT stable for many years now. You will read about their evolutions in the following chapters. Having lived them as both an analyst and investor, I can say they emerged from very different circumstances, but the common threads remained the same: differentiation, better customer service, and a refusal to stand still.

In the years since I first met Kirk, JBHT has done its thing from the inside: natural expansion with homegrown talent. This has worked like nothing I have seen in all my years in the investment business. Yet, curiously, the company has made one of its most recent senior hires from the outside. What's on its mind? Possibly the next evolution in logistics for the e-commerce world? I don't know, but rest assured, the field of purple cows is going to broaden.

I believe strongly not only in what JBHT has accomplished, but also in how it got there. There's much to absorb within these pages. If I am a corporate executive, I want to aspire to the characteristics and discipline that drives this company. If I am an investor, I want to invest in companies that manage and perform in this fashion. If I am a student of business, I want to study how the company yoked theory to common sense to produce such strong long-term results. *Purple on the Inside* presents a fascinating portrait of the changes within a vital American industry through the achievements of one of its most successful companies.

Enjoy.

Gary Yablon
Managing Partner, Impala Asset Management

ACKNOWLEDGMENTS

This might seem a bit strange, but we're going to open the acknowledgments of this book by quoting from a couple of its passages.

As you make your way through the pages, you'll read where we describe J.B. Hunt Transport as a "story of leaders and team members who built a culture that tapped into the founder's spirit for innovation while bringing the focus and execution the company needed to grow."

You'll also come across this line: "Throughout the evolution that brings us to today, the people at JBHT have been the difference in capitulation to difficulty versus pushing through to decisive success."

Furthermore, you'll see terms like *team, people,* and *culture* repeated over and over.

The story of this book is much like the story of J.B. Hunt Transport—it is the result of the work of many individuals collaborating as a team to create something much greater than any of us could have accomplished on our own. So, as the authors whose names go on the front of the book, we want take a moment to say thanks to those who helped make it possible.

First, we're thankful to our families, who supported us, encouraged us, and didn't complain when we took time to work on this project.

We're also thankful to the teams of people at the University of Arkansas and at J.B. Hunt Transport who contributed and/or assisted in collecting information, providing interviews, reviewing copy, and in many other ways supporting this project along the way.

Lori Foster, the assistant to the dean at the Walton College of Business, was critical in keeping things organized and scheduling interviews. And while the list of people who allowed us to interview them is long, it's worth sharing. The current or former JBHT employees we interviewed include Paul Bergant, Mark Greenway, Craig Harper, Nick Hobbs, John Roberts, Stuart Scott, and Shelley Simpson. And industry experts who contributed include John Larkin, Andy Petery, and Gary Yablon (who wrote the foreword).

This book was published by EPIC Books, a new imprint created in collaboration between the University of Arkansas Press and the Walton College of Business. So, we're thankful to Mike Bieker, the director of the University of Arkansas Press, for shepherding that collaboration and helping make this book the inaugural publication for the imprint. Thanks to Mike, too, for his expert developmental editing. A big thanks goes out to Stephen Caldwell who kept the project on track and worked with us to wordsmith the manuscript.

As we close, there's one other line in the book that's worth noting: "If you ain't got no animals, you ain't hardly got no circus." This book had the right animals and, we think, produced an amazing circus. We hope you enjoy reading it as much as we enjoyed writing it.

Kirk Thompson and Matthew A. Waller

Creating Purple Cows

The essence of the Purple Cow is that it must be remarkable.
—Seth Godin, author

We were having a casual conversation about the dramatic growth of J.B. Hunt Transport Services over the last fifteen to twenty years when it occurred to us that this story—one of the greatest American business success stories of all time—had never really been told, certainly not in a book.

Plenty has been written about how Johnnie Bryan Hunt rose from rural Cleburne County, Arkansas, during the Depression era and co-founded the company that bears his name. J.B. and his wife, Johnelle, started out in the rice-hull packing business, before helping build what would become one of the largest publicly owned trucking companies in the country. And the couple left an indelible legacy that reaches far beyond the world of business. They laid the foundations for the company's corporate giving programs, and Johnelle, who was active in the company as its corporate secretary until 2008 and is still the largest shareholder, remains involved in real estate ventures and philanthropic efforts.

But the story often focuses on the legendary founder, it typically ends not long after the company went public in 1983, and it never connects J.B. Hunt Transport's growth and success to the underlying business theories that were and are at work. Thus, many of the powerful, valuable, and transferable lessons from the company's story remain untold.

This book will change that.

The fact is, there's much more to the story of J.B. Hunt Transport than meets the eye. And that's what makes it both fascinating and influential. From the highs and lows, successes and failures, JBHT has emerged as an industry leader—and not just in trucking. But to fully understand, appreciate, and learn from this story, you have to go beyond the obvious and look at what's hidden inside. That's where you'll find something truly unexpected. Something, well . . . purple.

Purple? . . . On the inside?

That's J.B. Hunt Transport—a company whose growth and success are tied to its ability to reinvent itself with purple cow business segments that distinguish the company from its brown cow competition.

Allow us to explain.

A Marketer's Metaphor

Imagine for a minute that you are Seth Godin, the best-selling author and marketing guru. You're cruising down a country road when the brown cows that dot the rolling hillsides suddenly inspire the metaphor for your next book. Brown cows, you've realized, quickly go from interesting to boring. And boring stuff—even when it's excellent—quickly becomes invisible. But a purple cow in a field of ordinary brown cows? Now that would stand out. It would get your attention.

You'll call the book *The Purple Cow,* and it will represent the idea that organizations must market not only great products, but products that stand out from the crowd. You'll point out that the old ways of marketing and advertising no longer are good enough. And you'll suggest some new ideas for making a product stand out. Go forth, you'll then say, and make your products, services, and brand a purple cow!

What you don't realize—or, if you do, what you don't address in your book—is that a purple cow can, at first glance, look very much like all the brown cows. If you're glancing at it through your window as you speed down the highway, it might not look different at all. It's only when you stop for a closer look that you realize the seemingly ordinary is, in fact, extraordinary.

If you've read Godin's book since it debuted in 2003 and made a list of purple cow companies, it probably didn't include J.B. Hunt Transport Services. But spend a few minutes studying the field known as the freight transportation industry. The cows all look the same, because they pretty much are all the same—especially in the trucking sector. That's where you see J.B. Hunt Transport, or so you think. It's one of the dominant players in the truckload trucking industry, after all, and man oh man is that an industry filled with brown cows.

J.B. Hunt Transport is a market leader in truckload trucking despite owning less than 3 percent of the U.S. market share. That's because there are more than 1.25 million trucking companies in America, but 97 percent of them operate fewer than twenty trucks.[1]

The result? Brown cow. Brown cow. Brown cow. Brown cow. Brown cow. Brown cow. Brown cow. Brown cow. Brown cow. Brown cow. Brown cow. Brown cow. Brown cow. Brown cow. Brown cow. Brown cow. Brown cow. . . .

You get the idea.

Of course, there is nothing inherently wrong with brown cows. You can feed them, inoculate them, and pasture them in the best location and environment, and they'll typically do just fine. But all you wind up with is brown cows that are not much different from any other herd of brown cows in the world.

It's understandable if, at first glance, JBHT appears to be just one of many brown cows among many brown cow herds. Then you look a little closer and you see the purple. It's not on the outside. It's not flashy like a shoe company or tech startup or Beyoncé. But it's there. On the inside. It draws you closer until you realize this mundane company in this boring industry is, in fact, not what you thought. It's not even a trucking company. It's a logistics services company. And while that at first might seem equally nondescript, the inner purple glow alerts you to something different.

That glow tells you this no longer is just a company that moves freight; this is a company that makes freight move. It tells you this is no longer just a company driven by men and women in truck cabs; it's a company driven by big data and insights. It tells you, as Chief Information Officer Stuart Scott likes to put it, this no longer is an assets company that uses technology; it's a technology company that uses assets. It tells you the magic of this company isn't found in the obvious, it's found in a unique culture that consistently develops innovative and disruptive ideas—ideas that have taken JBHT from an ordinary player in an overcrowded field and turned it into a one-of-a-kind success story.

Purple on the Inside tells the story of how J.B. Hunt Transport transformed itself into a multi-billion-dollar business by truly setting itself apart from its competition.

---

1. Available at http://www.trucking.org/News_and_Information_Reports _Industry_Data.aspx, accessed May 14, 2018.

JBHT's corporate colors are black and yellow, but you'll see the purple when you look at three key aspects of the business — Intermodal, Dedicated Contract Services (DCS), and Integrated Capacity Solutions (ICS). JBHT got into those businesses well before most of its competition and developed partnerships, technologies, and expertise that others can't easily duplicate. Those units, in fact, now far outpace truckload trucking as the company's primary sources of revenue and profitability. And you will see the purple in the rising influence of technology within the engine of the business. Not only is JBHT setting the pace when it comes to applying advanced technologies like radio frequency identification (RFID) or powering trucks with electric engines, but we also are developing software for the entire supply chain industry and operating a cloud-based platform for drivers, shippers, and customers.

The story of J.B. Hunt Transport, therefore, is far more than a story of a dynamic, entrepreneurial founder who built a business largely on boundless optimism and salesmanship. It's a story of leaders and team members who built a culture that tapped into the founder's spirit for innovation while bringing the focus and execution the company needed to grow. And it's a story of how that culture overcame disheartening setbacks and cultivated the distinctive qualities that allow J.B. Hunt Transport to do what most experts said was impossible — stand out.

When you look even closer, though, you'll see that it's also a story of how business theory, leadership, and organizational best practices played out during the company's growth. This often happened unintentionally. JBHT wasn't building a company from some business theory playbook. Craig Harper, who joined JBHT in 1992 and now is executive vice president, put it this way: "We did a lot of things right that we didn't even know were right. The books are telling you they were the right thing to do now. And you look back and say, 'We did that. We just didn't know that we were doing that.'"

Like many successful companies, J.B. Hunt Transport is the product of a lot of smart, hard-working people who made decisions primarily based on intuition, common sense, and deeply held values. So, we'll look at how JBHT developed and maintains a culture that encourages and supports innovative best practices and decisions. And, in retrospect, we can connect those decisions and strategies to business theories in ways that allow current and future leaders to apply them with more intentionality. We'll look at the role things like barriers to entry, options pricing theory, decision theory, creative destruction, systems theory, and core competency played in creating these purple cow segments. We'll weave those business principles through the milestone moments in the company's history. This makes it a story rich with lessons that apply to any business and any leader in any industry.

So, what you'll find in the pages to come is a corporate history that connects real stories from a real business to the theories that often are taught in university classrooms all around the world. For students, it's a rare opportunity to see how such theories have played out and, more important, how to make use of them once you enter the job market. For leaders already in the business world, especially those at JBHT, it's also an opportunity to appreciate what's worked while learning how to intentionally drive better strategic decisions that will set you and your organization up for success.

Our Voice(s)

Note: As co-authors, we had to decide how to express our voices in this book. One of us (Matt) is the dean of a business college with a deep background in supply chain management and who has followed and worked with JBHT for more than two decades. The other (Kirk) literally lived the story of JBHT, joining the company in 1973 before he even graduated from college. He went on to lead the company as CEO from 1987 through 2010, and he has been chairman of the board since 2010.

Needless to say, we bring very different skill sets, experiences, and insights to this project. As you might imagine, many of Kirk's contributions are in the stories he witnessed or that he asked others to share, while Matt's contributions tend to focus on research and connecting the story of JBHT to the various business theories. Generally, we found a first-person plural voice worked well in bringing our voices together. But since much of the storytelling comes from Kirk's decades of personal experience with JBHT, the first-person singular voice you read along the way belongs to him.

CHAPTER 1

Where Now, Brown Cow?

When you come to a fork in the road, take it.
— Yogi Berra, former baseball player

Yogi Berra once invited his friend Joe Garagiola to visit him at his home in New Jersey. Joe agreed, so he asked Yogi for directions. Yogi, of course, obliged in his uniquely Yogi Berra way. And during his description of how to get from Point A (New York City) to Point B (Montclair, N.J.), Yogi offered up his now famous directive: "When you come to a fork in the road, take it."

We've all been there, right? We face the choices of life and somehow want to take every available option. We don't want to miss something. We'd like to think there's a right road and the others are bad, but sometimes several options are good—or at least interesting.

It's that last scenario that was taking J.B. Hunt Transport Services—a company that knew a thing or two about navigating roads—toward the proverbial ditch. How ironic that a company that owed so much of its success to taking risks and trying new ideas faced an uncertain future because it struggled to focus on where it really needed to go.

As the president and CEO of the company, I knew we had come to the fork in the road and that we had, indeed, taken it. We were headed to some great places, but we also were headed toward some obvious dead ends. We were pretty much headed everywhere—all at the same time.

That's when I got the news that changed our course.

I was sitting in my fourth-floor office before a board meeting in 1995, wondering, frankly, how I was going to make it through another day. My enthusiasm for my job as CEO had reached an all-time low, and, much as I hate to admit it, I had begun to dread coming to work. I didn't like where the company was heading, and I wasn't sure how to change our direction. It wasn't a good feeling.

Wayne Garrison wasn't happy, either. Wayne had preceded me as CEO, and now he was a member of the company's board of directors. His first stop that day was the office of Johnnie Bryan Hunt, the company's co-founder and namesake. J.B., who started the company with his wife, Johnelle, in 1961, was chairman of the board and the company's largest shareholder.

J.B.'s "Horatio Alger story" is well known, especially in trucking business lore. He was born February 28, 1927, in the rural mountains of north Arkansas, raised during the Great Depression, and eventually became one of the state's "big six" industrial icons along with Wal-Mart founder Sam Walton, Tyson Foods founder John W. Tyson, Stephens Inc. founders Jack and Witt Stephens, and Dillard's founder Bill Dillard. Those men all built companies that would end up among the most successful ever in their respective industries.

J.B. never advanced in school beyond the seventh grade and worked several odd jobs early in his adult life—in a sawmill, selling lumber, as an auctioneer. He was a truck driver in 1961 when he and Johnelle launched The J.B. Hunt Company, which, when you think about it, was a recycling business *way* before recycling was cool. In those days, rice hulls were processing waste. Some farmers burned them in the fields. Rice mills paid $1 a ton to have them hauled off. J.B. realized the hulls had value to poultry farmers as litter, so he designed a first-of-its-kind machine to pack the fluffy hulls so they could be shipped and sold to poultry farmers in the northwest corner of Arkansas and beyond. Then he convinced investors—primarily Arkansas companies and individuals—to help fund his big idea.

"The first year we were in business, we lost $19,000," Johnelle Hunt said. "And all the accountants and all the people we were working with were saying you'll have to close the doors. You can't go on. . . . We had to make this work. We just kept going. We just kept working."[1]

The hard work paid off. The rice-hull packing business became profitable in its second year, and the company eventually transformed into a giant in the truckload trucking industry.

Wayne and I were among the first employees hired after the Hunts moved to northwest Arkansas in the 1970s, transitioned into trucking, and eventually

---

1. "J.B. Hunt Origins 1927–1990," available at www.youtube.com/watch?v =TjfHchzNuQY, accessed August 22, 2017.

sold off the rice-hull business. When I started as a minimum wage hand in the accounting department in 1973, I still hadn't finished my college degree. I was driving a 1964 Oldsmobile that later was crashed into by a runaway J.B. Hunt rice-hull truck in the parking lot. Since the Olds was like a tank, I just collected the insurance money, overlooked the dents, and had a better-than-expected Christmas that year.

In the late 1970s, we began operating in some unique ways that separated us from our competition, especially once our industry was deregulated in 1980. We standardized our trucking fleet, for instance, using smaller, more efficient engines to save on fuel costs. We also hired company drivers instead of independent contractors, and we had policies such as dress codes to champion them as professionals. Our employees, meanwhile, excelled in the three critical elements of running a trucking company: (1) utilization of productivity. Miles per truck per day was the metric we used. (2) keeping "empty miles" as low as possible. And, (3) minimizing costs.

We had phenomenal earnings for a small company. Our financial performance attracted the attention of investment banks, including Stephens Inc., the Little Rock-based financial services firm. Stephens handled the initial offering along with Alex. Brown & Sons of Baltimore, taking Hunt public in 1983. That was the beginning of real financial success. During a time when hundreds of other truckload carriers went bankrupt, we seized the opportunity and raced to the top. But maintaining that success year over year was an increasingly difficult challenge. Andy Petery, one of the best analysts who covered the transportation industry before retiring from Morgan Stanley, says it was to be expected given J.B.'s personality and the demands the market put on the company.

"If you're a pioneer, which they were, you are going to encounter problems and criticism along the way, which they have," Andy told us. "Initially, there were some rocky times, because earnings did not meet expectations. The company was spending too much money."

Andy points out that J.B.'s focus on new ideas that took time to develop (or fade away) was consistent with the long-term thinking often found in countries like China, but it didn't always sit well with the microwave-like expectations of investors in America.

"In other words, he had a different horizon from what we would have on Wall Street," Andy said. "And the tension was always, 'When will he deliver earnings? So, it was really a transition from a private enterprise to a public company, and the harvesting of the creative energy of a great visionary thinker, J.B. Hunt, and managing the public market's expectations. That was the source of the tension in the initial years."

As time wore on, competitors throughout the industry began catching up. Many of our innovative best practices in truckload were easily emulated by others, and some of our competitors also increased their capitalization by going public. Like other trucking companies, we battled the never-ending challenge to recruit and keep great drivers. The national economy delivered multiple recessions. And the trucking industry had almost become a commodity, with no company finding a way to distinguish itself from the pack. Frankly, we had an impatient founder who wanted to maintain the frantic growth rate at all cost. In an effort to innovate and continue that growth, we often found ourselves chasing a variety of business rabbits—some good, some not so good, and some horrible.

John Larkin, an analyst with Stifel Transportation and Logistics Research Group, was part of the Alex. Brown & Sons team when we went public, and he remembers the double-edged sword that came with having such a creative-minded founder.

"You had an entrepreneur without much formal education who didn't care to get too involved in the details of the plan," John said. "He wanted to assign somebody to make it happen. He had to come up with another idea tomorrow. He was one of the all-time great idea generators. He might have had a hundred ideas and four of them ended up being pretty darn good. The vast preponderance of the others was shot down before they became reality."

Our growth began to stall around 1987, which, ironically, was the year I became CEO at the tender age of 34. We did $286 million in revenue that year, but we were beginning to feel the tensions that came with a changing market, demanding shareholders, and a visionary founder. On the turning-point day of that board meeting in 1995, the outlook wasn't promising. That's when Wayne told J.B. he didn't like the direction the company was headed and he planned to sell his stock and move on with life.

J.B., who by then was nearly seventy, wasn't one to let go. Indeed, that was part of the problem. His larger-than-life personality had helped inspire much of the company's success, but our continued growth depended on more than a sanguine personality with a million big ideas and the passion to sell them. J.B.'s single-minded drive for growth had prompted us to take on risky investments and ventures that led to a lack of focus on the fundamentals of our business.

To his credit, however, J.B. knew things weren't going well and that he wasn't sure how to fix them. So, he implored Wayne to stay involved.

"I'll do it on one condition," Wayne told him. "You retire, leave, and don't meddle."

Wayne's next stop was my office. He told me J.B. had agreed to retire, and, frankly, I was relieved. It's a little tough to say that now, because I don't want to seem disrespectful of J.B.—there would be no J.B. Hunt Transport Services without Johnnie Bryan Hunt. But I was thankful that he'd shown the courage and wisdom to do what was best for the company. I often say, "Don't stay too long at the dance." I've witnessed successful people overstay at their positions as the demands outpace their impressive abilities. Know when to pass the baton! And I was thankful because I knew this change would allow for some important and much-needed shifts in our corporate direction.

Wayne would replace J.B. as chairman of the board, and he and I were extraordinarily well-aligned when it came to business philosophy. We agreed on what needed to be done and we believed we could execute. The transition was not immediate nor was it painless. There were a lot of excuses for the less-than-stellar financial results from 1987 through 1994, but it was out of those dark years that a new and bigger success story was born. J.B. Hunt Transport went from primarily a truckload carrier that had $286 million in revenues in 1987 to a logistics services provider with $3.8 billion in revenues by 2010.

How did we do it?

We stopped driving down every fork in every road, and we focused on the ones where we could see a purple cow.

In the years prior to J.B.'s retirement as chairman of the board, JBHT toyed with or actually got into a number of businesses. J.B., for instance, wanted to build a huge airport in northwest Arkansas that would be the air freight hub of the nation. That never happened. He wanted the computer system in our new headquarters to process every truckload transaction in the country. That never happened, either. We looked at manufacturing our own trailers and buying a trucking company in Spain. Those things never happened, either.

We did, however, purchase Bulldog Trucking, a flatbed carrier based in Georgia. That didn't work out for us. And we built prototypes of containers and trailers with a specialized rack inside so that they could double-stack and haul automobiles. The idea was that a trailer or container could carry freight to one location, then be available to carry automobiles for the return trip (or vice versa). J.B. referred to it as the "Eighth Wonder of the World," but the concept ultimately failed. We started two companies, QXI and LXI, that were designed to be smaller and less strapped by corporate overhead. In theory, they would operate more creatively and nimbly. Both enterprises lasted only a few years.

All of these ventures were beneficial, if only for the lessons learned along the way. But not long after Wayne became chairman of the board, we realized it was time to do what one financial analyst often referred to as "chopping wood." But to stick with the metaphor of this book, let's just say we needed to get rid of some of our brown cows—business segments that struggled or that did fine but didn't have much potential for standing out.

Craig Harper, who came to JBHT in 1992, was running our Special Commodities segment during that time, and it was one of several business segments that qualified as a brown cow.

"When Wayne Garrison came back in 1995, he interviewed all of us and he asked me if [special commodities] could get to be a billion dollars," Harper recalled. "I'm gonna guess we were somewhere around $50 million. I'm thinking, 'There's no way in hell we can be a billion dollars.' He said, 'Well, then you need to find something else to do, because you're nothing but a distraction. If you can't get it to a billion dollars, we need to sell it.'"

In the months and years to follow, we shut down or sold off the segments we didn't see as a potential purple cow. That eventually left us with a focus on Intermodal, Dedicated Contract Services (DCS), and Integrated Capacity Solutions (ICS), all of which were built on the foundation of the truckload trucking business. What we *didn't* do was chop people. Craig is a prime example. He could have left, but we valued what he brought to JBHT and he appreciated what we provided him. So, he migrated to new areas of the company and charged forward, making significant contributions and showing leadership in new responsibilities.

We also didn't lose our entrepreneurial spirit. That term gets tossed around rather loosely in business. For us, it means that we found a way to build a culture of great people who capture the creative and innovative heart of our founder, manage with some practical restraints of good business, and use the resulting platform as a springboard for growth and profitability. It means that as long as we hire, train, and retain great people who embody that spirit, we'll always be a bit unpredictable, but we will find ourselves moving toward something greater, and we'll enjoy the journey together.

Timeline:
J.B. Hunt Transport History with Economic Context

Pre-1960s

1935   Interstate Commerce Commission established, regulates trucking industry.

1960s

1961   The J.B. Hunt Company is incorporated in Arkansas on August 10 as an agricultural supply and rice-hull packing business. In its first year in business, the company lost $19,123 on revenues of $50,626.

1962   Stuttgart rice-hull packing plant opens at a cost of $100,000.

1962   Wal-Mart Stores Inc. founded.

1969   By end of the decade, the J.B. Hunt Company is the largest rice-hull dealer in the nation.

1969   The company reports revenue of $827,198 and profit of $51,550; enters the trucking industry by purchasing five old trucks and seven worn-out refrigerated trailers.

1970s

1971   FedEx Corp. founded.

1973   Kirk Thompson joins J.B. Hunt as a minimum-wage employee.

1975   Microsoft Corp. founded.

1976   Apple Computer Co. founded.

1978   China begins economic liberalization.

1978   Acquisition of E.L. Reddish Transportation allows JBHT to expand to thirty-three states, adds twenty-four trucks.

1979   By late 1970s, ICC begins to loosen approvals, JBHT gets 90 percent of its applications to haul freight approved. Trucks to West Coast.

1979   J.B. Hunt reports revenues of $14.7 million, net income is $564,000.

1980s

1980   Federal Motor Carrier Act of 1980 deregulates trucking industry. JBHT able to obtain unlimited authority to carry general commodities throughout the forty-eight contiguous states.

1980   J.B. Hunt reports $10,000 loss on revenues of $6.98 million.

1981   The Economic Recovery Tax Act is signed into law.

1983   J.B. Hunt sells rice-hull operation in Stuttgart, Arkansas, to Eli Lilly for $2 million in cash.

1983   JBHT initial public offering in November: 1.32 million shares sold and net proceeds $18.5 million, priced at $18.75 a share.

1983   Wayne Garrison becomes president of JBHT.

1984   Arkansas Department of Finance charges JBHT with failure to pay $521,122 in sales and use taxes; company loses case in January 23 hearing.

1987   The Dow Jones drops 508 points (20.4 percent) on "Black Monday" (October 19); at the time, the greatest single-day loss in Wall Street history.

1987   Kirk Thompson becomes president and CEO of JBHT (1987 to 2011).

1988   JBHT receives Canadian authority to ship.

1989   World Wide Web invented by Tim Berners-Lee.

1989   JBHT provides transportation services to and from Mexico.

1989   JBHT begins a "strategic alliance" with the Santa Fe Railway Company, the first successful venture in intermodal transportation between the rival industries.

1990s

1990   JBHT finishes and moves into a 150,000-square-foot headquarters building.

1991   Flatbed, special commodities operations created.

1992   JBHT announces a joint venture with Transportacion Maritima Mexicana, the largest transportation company in Mexico.

1992   JBHT acquires small hazardous waste carrier.

1992   JBHT pays a three-for-two stock split (March 13).

1992   JBHT begins offering transportation logistics services and dedicated contract services.

1993 New hazardous waste unit begins operation.

1993 JBHT expands joint truck and rail in Canada with Canadian National railroad.

1993 On December 31, J.B. Hunt employed 10,476 people, including 7,531 drivers, and operated 6,775 tractors and 19,089 trailers/containers.

1994 Netscape Communications founded.

1995 J.B. Hunt retires from the trucking business, but remains on board until 2004.

1995 S&P reduces domestic long-term credit rating from A to A- (March 31).

1995 Stock loses 6 cents a share (EPS); first and only negative annual return.

1996 JBHT concentrates on dry van, logistics, dedicated contract units; sells off parcel, hazardous waste business. It also builds new terminal and maintenance facility in Chicago.

1996 S&P reduces domestic long-term credit rating from A- to BBB+ (October 31).

1997 Broadband Internet service arrives at homes.

1997 JBHT provides a 33 percent pay increase for 3,500 drivers (effective February 25).

1998 Google founded.

1998 On December 31, JBHT employed 14,250 people, including 10,500 drivers, and operated 8,900 tractors.

1999 JBHT builds new terminal and maintenance facility in Kansas City, Missouri.

2000s

2000 JBHT ends its logistics division; forms Transplace Inc. with five other companies; has a 27 percent share in the venture.

2001 S&P reduces domestic long-term credit rating from BBB+ to BBB (April 30).

2001 China joins World Trade Organization (WTO).

2001 Internet stock bubble bursts, ending a decade-long period of often laudatory business coverage; $8 trillion wealth evaporates.

2001 Al Qaeda terrorists attack World Trade Center and Pentagon on September 11, killing nearly 3,000 people.

2001   Enron fails.

2001   U.S. recession (March through November).

2002   JBHT ends joint venture in Mexico; sells interest in Mexico to Transportacion Maritima Mexicana (TMM).

2003   JBHT's largest customer, Wal-Mart Stores, Inc., accounts for 13 percent of total revenue.

2003   JBHT pays two-for-one stock split.

2003   On December 31, JBHT employed 15,700 people, including 11,600 drivers, and owned 9,935 tractors.

2004   J.B. Hunt steps down from the company board.

2004   S&P raises domestic long-term credit rating from BBB to BBB+ (May 31).

2005   JBHT board authorizes $500 million stock buyback over the next five years.

2005   Two-for-one stock split.

2005   JBHT's dry-van freight unit, JBT, reports $1.02 billion in revenues for calendar year.

2005   Arbitration settled between JBHT and BNSF Railway Company (BNI).

2007   U.S. recession starts in December (ends June 2009).

2007   S&P lowers domestic long-term credit rating from BBB+ to BBB (May 31).

2008   Congress passes $700 billion TARP rescue bailout.

2008   On December 31, JBHT employed 14,667 people, including 10,022 drivers, and owned 9,067 tractors.

2010S

2011   John N. Roberts III elected as president and CEO effective January 1; Kirk Thompson remains chairman of the board.

2011   Federal hourly service rules affect productivity. In 2011, the FMCSA amended the hours-of-service (HOS) safety requirements for commercial truck drivers.

2011   China overtakes Japan to become the world's second-largest economy ($5.8 trillion).

2012   S&P raises domestic long-term credit rating from BBB to BBB+ (July 31).

2013   On December 31, JBHT employed 18,467 people, including 12,632 drivers, and owned 10,453 tractors.

2014 JBHT incorporates reducing greenhouse gas emissions as part of its business strategy offerings.

2014 Launched the J.B. Hunt Experience, a long-term cultural enhancement initiative to create a better working environment and service culture among customers, drivers, maintenance, and office employees.

2014 Launched J.B. Hunt 360, a web-based, mobile-friendly service that allows customers to obtain rate quotes, book services, trace load progress, and pay using credit cards.

2014 Total consolidated operating revenue exceeded $6 billion, operating income improved to more than $630 million, and earnings per share rose to $3.16.

2015 At year's end, JBHT employed 21,500 people, owned 12,500 tractors, 29,247 trailers, 78,986 containers, and 68,076 chassis. JBHT also owned or leased forty-two terminal facilities, eighty-nine Final Mile Services cross-dock locations, thirty-four ICS branch sales offices, and other support locations across the United States, Canada, and Mexico.

2015 Stuart Scott is named JBHT's new chief information officer and executive vice president of technology and engineering.

2017 JBHT announces a five-year $500 million investment into "innovative and disruptive" technologies.

2017 JBHT announces plans to purchase electric-powered tractors from Tesla Motors for use with its DCS operations on the West Coast.

2017 JBHT acquires Houston-based Special Logistics Dedicated for $136 million.

2018 *Forbes* listed JBHT as one of America's Best Large Employers of 2018.

2018 Inbound Logistics named JBHT as a Top 10 3PL for the ninth consecutive year.

2018 VIQTORY named JBHT a "Military Friendly Employer" for the twelfth consecutive year.

2018 JBHT awarded nearly $1 million in safe driver bonuses and recognized seventy-seven drivers who had achieved two, three, and four million safe miles driven within the past year. More than 3,400 drivers now have reached one million safe miles for the company.

2019 JBHT announces plans to buy Cory 1st Choice Home Delivery of New Jersey for $100 million.

CHAPTER 2

No Animals, No Circus

If the culture you have is radically different from an "experiment
and take-risk" culture, then you have a big change you are going to
have to make, and no little gimmicks are going to do it for you.
—John P. Kotter, author

'm a fan of hackneyed yet salient one-liners, and one in particular stands
out whenever I think about the importance of people to the success of J.B.
Hunt Transport: "If you ain't got no animals, you ain't hardly got no circus."

That line is often attributed to Casey Stengel, but I've always given credit
to Yogi Berra. Either way, the point is the same: People matter. Business gurus
like to say things like "people are your most important asset" or that "culture
eats strategy for breakfast." I can tell you from experience that the gurus, at
least in this case, are right! It might sound cliché, but JBHT owes its success
first and foremost to its people. Throughout the evolution that brings us to
today, the people at JBHT have been the difference in capitulation to difficulty
versus pushing through to decisive success. There have been many missteps
along the way, but JBHT has managed to hire and keep the right people, creating the type of loyalty and engagement that's essential to serving customers—
and developing distinctively purple cow business segments.

An excerpt from our 2015 "Letter to Shareholders" captures the basic philosophy that's been in place since the early days of the company:

> Every day in every part of the company, more than 21,500 of the most
> dedicated people in the transportation industry work with a passion and
> commitment to serve our customers and each other. Each of them helps
> to deliver on our promises that we will be safe and strive to create real
> value for our customers and our stockholders. Our culture encourages
> innovation and we embrace the services built on a growing foundation
> of industry-leading technology. So far, this combination of core princi-

ples has been at the center of our growth and sustainability. Every day, the good people of J.B. Hunt are working hard to build a bigger, stronger, and better company. We are very proud of them.

The cynic might read those words as mere corporate-speak, variants of which can be found in virtually any company's letter to shareholders. But there's no question that the success of JBHT is powered by the quality of its people and that the sustained success of JBHT rests in its ability to maintain a distinct culture that has remained committed to its core values while adapting to the new realities.

In the shareholders' statement, we employ words like "dedicated," "passion," and "commitment" to describe our team. We stress ideals like delivering on our promises, emphasizing safety, creating value for customers and stockholders, and embracing innovation and technology. As we will illustrate in this chapter and throughout this book, none of those are hollow descriptors. They are the DNA of the JBHT culture.

Make no mistake: Culture matters.

When other leaders ask how they can replicate the success of J.B. Hunt Transport, I'm quick to point out that there is no "silver bullet." There's a list of things like how you treat people, how you view the market, and how you communicate. Things that for the most part you can put under the header of a healthy "culture." That's what differentiates one company from another.

A culture is simply a shared way of thinking, behaving, or working based on the common beliefs and customs of an organization. Some parts of a culture are shaped and driven by proclamations handed down from on high like vision statements and lists of corporate values, but the real culture of any organization is revealed in the day-to-day way the people go about their business. It's not a mantra or tagline formulated in a boardroom, but a story written by the people who are living it. As we look at how this culture evolved from the early days, we can see how it's grown even better with time.

Dressed for Success

Visit the JBHT headquarters in Lowell, Arkansas, and you'll quickly notice the "business casual" atmosphere. Many employees wear jeans, but you won't see anyone who doesn't have a "professional" appearance. In some ways, we've come full circle.

When Paul Bergant joined our team in the late 1970s, he came from a law firm in Chicago. On his first day with JBHT, Paul arrived wearing a three-piece suit, just as you might expect from an attorney.

"I stood out like a well-dressed sore thumb," he said.

Trucking companies in those days were very blue collar—at all levels of the organizations. Even the corporate offices of trucking firms tended to be smoke-filled rooms manned (literally) by burly former truck drivers. But J.B., who was a boots-and-Stetson sort of man, recognized an opportunity for the company to set itself apart from the competition by cultivating a more professional atmosphere, both at the corporate level and with our drivers. Soon, suits and ties became the norm for the men at headquarters, and corporate drivers were required to wear uniforms and maintain a professional appearance while on the job. This made a positive impression on existing and potential customers. And our employees began to see themselves as professionals, which changed the way they thought about each other and their work.

"It helped the people who were trying to drive the change," Paul told us. "It gave us a sense of identity that we felt like we needed to have a chance to prove ourselves."

Over time, however, the environment grew a bit "sterile," as Craig Harper described it. Craig had worked for several other companies before joining JBHT in 1992. Not only did the men wear coats and ties when he arrived, but there were restrictions on things like who could use the intercom system, how many family photos you could have on your desk, and even what kind of coffee cup you could have on your desk.

"A lot of these things were done for the right reasons," he said, "but things evolved."

They began to change in 1995 when Wayne Garrison, the former CEO, returned as chairman of the board. Back then, the main mode of mass communication was what we called a "Group 70" message. It went out through the phone system, and employees called to hear the recorded message.

"I dialed in one day and heard that Wayne Garrison was the new chairman and that we were going to casual dress because Wayne only owned one suit," Craig recalled. "So, we went to casual dress."

Family Matters

Regardless of whether we've worn jeans, ties, or a uniform, the constant has become this: professional pride. It's something we stress with new employees, but more important it's become part of our cultural DNA.

The backbone of JBHT's culture is our long-term employees who lead by example and spread the cultural norms and expectations throughout their teams. One of our best decisions was to create a management training program in the early 1980s that helped fill the pipeline with bright, young future executives who have shaped and sustained the culture. The company was much smaller back then, and our top executives interviewed every candidate. Nick Hobbs was the third person to complete the program, and John Roberts followed shortly after he graduated from college. John, of course, is now JBHT's CEO, while Nick is an executive vice president.

"I was just going to do it until I could find something better," Nick said of taking a job with JBHT. "I haven't found anything better yet."

Coming up through the ranks of an organization has many advantages, particularly at JBHT. Outsiders can make it, but that path is not without disadvantages, struggles, and obstacles. That's why we've seldom done well with acquisitions or by depending too heavily on outside experts to run parts of our business. Of course, some "tuck-in" acquisitions complement a segment of our business and make sense. We won't pass on a good fit, but, for the most part, the JBHT body tends to reject organ donations.

The most obvious example of this comes from our Dedicated Contract Services. We hired an outside group to start DCS because we lacked the internal expertise to launch that business. Right off the bat, we made two mistakes. First, the DCS team operated out of Atlanta rather than Arkansas. And, second, its leaders maintained a different pay and bonus structure from the other JBHT leaders.

When we decided they needed to operate in alignment with the rest of the company, the DCS team rebelled. Resignation letters from the nineteen top leaders of DCS, all of whom had been external hires, jammed our fax machine. It was a power play, but we weren't interested in the game. We let them go. John, who had been our top DCS salesman, received a battlefield promotion that we will discuss in more detail later, and it was under his leadership that DCS grew into a purple cow segment. Ultimately, we were better off for the departures since the individuals didn't share our values; if they had stayed, DCS may have never aligned with the company.

When Shelley Simpson pulled together a team to launch Integrated Capacity Solutions (ICS) in 2007, she recognized the need for outside help, but she was wise enough not to allow us to become overly dependent on it. Shelley built her top-level leadership team with internal hires, focusing on men and women with reputations for flexibility and vision. The next level of management was an even mixture of internal and external candidates.

"We'd coach and train culture with the people from the outside, and we'd coach and train the business of brokerage to the people from the inside," Shelley said.

The external hires had to learn that JBHT wasn't a non-asset company like most freight brokerage companies. A tenant of the JBHT culture is to be what Shelley calls "modal indifferent." This means you do what makes the most sense for meeting the customer's needs even if that means using a different part of the company to accomplish the goals. ICS, for instance, can't hoard business that needs to go to Intermodal, which wasn't something outsiders quickly embraced when she was launching ICS.

"We can provide the best part of everything," she would tell them. "If you only look at it through the lens of being a broker, you'll miss the best parts of the company."

Selling JBHT, as opposed to one segment, results in more satisfied and loyal customers. Our bonus structure rewards leaders based on the company's overall performance. When the company performs well as a whole, everyone reaps the rewards.

Ironically, one of the things the original DCS leaders rebelled against was that bonus structure. There are legitimate arguments to do it other ways, but we find our approach fosters a one-for-all-and-all-for-one mentality. We incentivize the company's success, not just the success of any one part of it. Sharing the wealth with those who helped create it has worked for JBHT for nearly forty years. The bonus plan has remained the same for all that time with only minor tweaks.

The bonus plan and our long-term incentive (LTI) programs, which have been in place since we went public, are key parts of our success. The LTIs are stock ownership programs like stock options and restricted stock. More than a hundred people are covered under these plans. We call it our "Give a Crud" group. LTI is and has been a fundamental piece of our compensation. It's far more important, in our view, than the bonus. It causes everyone to think and act like an owner.

Mark Greenway, our senior vice president for human resources, points out that creating a modern equity compensation model that stretches all the way to the director level has been critical to our low turnover among leadership.

"That really unified the whole management team on a single focus and not just our bonus plan," he said. "And it pretty much eliminated turnover among top management. You look around J.B. Hunt and you see people like myself who have been here twenty or thirty years all over the place. There's not much turnover in the management team."

We're a performance-based culture, but we also realize quality returns look different in different areas of the business. We measure the quality of a team's results against its peer groups, not against other JHBT units, so we put the emphasis on being "best in class" not "best within JBHT." We've found that this helps eliminate the popularity contests, leads to better decisions, and allows us to celebrate contributions that otherwise might get overlooked.

"Culturally, we have continued to build on the idea that we're all part of the family," John points out. "Whether you're winning today or losing today, there's a brother or sister somewhere who's going to help pick up the slack."

For instance, our Truck segment did better than expected in 2014, generating roughly $6 million more income than we had forecast. Now, Truck represented less than 10 percent of our overall operating income of $700 million to $800 million, so that extra $6 million could get lost in the spreadsheets. But we saw it as a reason to celebrate. DCS fell short of its goal that year, and the extra $6 million from Truck enabled the company to meet our financial goals.

"You guys got us over the finish line," John told the folks in Truck. "You guys are the reason we won this year. It's not because Intermodal made $350 million, but because you guys made an extra $6 million. Your six made the difference."

John knows we compete as a team and everyone's contribution matters.

"You would have thought those guys won the Super Bowl," John told us. "They felt like they contributed. They were part of the team."

This illustrates a key part of our leadership direction—the portfolio effect. In investment circles, the portfolio effect represents a "reduction in the variation of returns on a combination of assets compared with the average of the variations of the individual assets."[1] We have a primary competitor in Intermodal, one in ICS, and one in DCS, and several in Truck. But as a collection of segments, we stand out. This allows us the opportunity to leverage the portfolio effect from a financial perspective, as in John's example. It also gives us the ability to deliver more value to customers. Simply having the capabilities that each segment offers, however, is not enough for the collection of the whole to deliver more value. That also requires the right culture—the alignment and motivation of our employees so that we can use this collection of capabilities in ways that deliver the services customers need.

A Culture of Promise

One of the great strengths of JBHT is its culture of promise.

Paul, for instance, remembers arriving in Northwest Arkansas in the 1970s when we were recruiting him to join our team. He met J.B. for the first time, and our founder cast his vision for the future as he drove Paul and his wife around the region, which, at the time, consisted mainly of pastures. Paul quickly realized he was joining a team that wasn't afraid of change but, instead, embraced it and rewarded those who worked hard and contributed to the company's success.

"Over the years, people who liked that idea migrated to our company," Paul said. "It's an opportunity for growth and an opportunity to experience new things. Then it feeds on itself. Growth comes from bright college kids and from great people in the industry who gravitate to it. We attracted people who were not stuck in their ways, who were going with the leading edge and in some cases creating leading edge. That's what you want in the business."

J.B. Hunt Transport has grown with the region. The four-county Metropolitan Statistical Area that makes up Northwest Arkansas had a population of around 80,000 when Paul came for that interview; now it's more than 525,000 and still growing. And because JBHT is growing with the times, there's plenty of opportunity for upward mobility. In DCS, for instance, our account managers average three-to-ten years of tenure, operations managers average around ten years of tenure, directors nearly fifteen years of tenure, and vice presidents

1. Financial Dictionary, FreeDictionary.com, http://financial-dictionary.thefree dictionary.com/portfolio+effect, accessed August 2, 2017.

at least fifteen years of tenure. The work is tough and the hours long, but, as Nick points out, "we pay well, there's a good bonus structure, and you can kind of control your destiny. And when we grow, there's lots of upward mobility. That's the reason we have a lot of tenure."

Nick rightly describes our culture as a unique alignment that focuses on listening to our customers and caring for our employees.

"So, our culture is all about training our employees to exceed our customers' expectations and then equipping them to do that," Nick said. "Then we have fun along the way, because we have a lot of success and a lot of growth."

Work is not supposed to be drudgery. I always advise young people, including my own children, to find a career path you enjoy, that makes you happy. You will excel at things you like, and life is too short to be mired in work you don't enjoy. We've tried to do our best to make JBHT a place where people are challenged to work hard but where they also can enjoy the journey. And our growth energizes our culture and allows us to sustain momentum by finding the right animals for our little circus.

"People can come here and stay here and promote," Nick said. "If we didn't have growth, we wouldn't have promotions. There would be stagnation all the way up. The key is growth. As John says, growth is an oxygen. That's what keeps us going. But if we take care of our customers and our people, the bottom line will always take care of itself."

CHAPTER 3

Life in Our Circus

You have to maintain a culture of transformation and stay true
to your values. — Jeff Weiner, CEO of LinkedIn

L eaders at all levels must understand their role in sustaining JBHT's distinctive culture. When I look back on the company's history, I see evidence of changes to our culture and examples of where we made mistakes, but also things we've done consistently that helped create a culture that
successfully stays true to some timeless values while adapting to the ever-
changing times:

- The leadership has always genuinely cared for the employees and their
  families. It's a legacy that began with J.B. and Johnelle Hunt, and it's
  lived out today by CEO John Roberts and his executive team.
- When we've established policies and strategic directions (like a commitment to safety), we've backed them fully from the top down with
  words as well as with visible actions.
- We've articulated simple and clear expectations.
- We've kept our promises. As a history professor once told me, "People
  don't revolt because things are bad. They revolt because they have been
  promised things are going to get better but they don't." Staying true to
  our word creates trust and credibility, which is critical not only with
  employees but with investors, vendors, and customers.
- We have remained entrepreneurial; we empower people to achieve
  great things without constructing obstacles that would impede creativity, independent thought, or clear vision.
- We have recognized and rewarded employees who do things the right
  way. That includes short- and long-term financial rewards, but it also
  includes things like publicly sharing success stories, attributing credit
  to those who earned it, and allowing leaders the freedom they need to
  run their parts of the business.

- We have valued collaboration. One-man shows are for carnivals or hot dog stands, not corporate America.
- We've been willing to change directions or policies that aren't working.

Those things have played out in various ways. You see them, for instance, in the way we've paid drivers, in our bonus structure for managers and leaders, in our benefits programs, in our dress codes, in our training programs, and in the ways we interact with customers. They are evident in the systems we create, the way we celebrate successes, and the grace we exhibit when things go poorly.

What's unique is that variables like time, growth, and the influx of new people haven't caused an erosion of our culture. Instead, they have added to it and strengthened it. We've been open to change, while staying true to our core; flexible enough to stretch with new ideas, but solid enough to maintain our identity. I credit this to the dynamic interplay between our culture and our leadership and management.

Leadership and management are simultaneously dependent on and responsible for the culture of an organization. Leadership is about dealing with change or driving change, whereas management is about dealing with complexity. John Kotter, the Harvard Business School professor who's written extensively on the subject, views leadership as being about setting direction, gaining alignment, and providing motivation. He views management as being about things like organizing, staffing, planning, budgeting, and controlling. Our leadership and management have always felt a deep obligation to care for the health of the culture. That mixture has allowed the culture to remain true to its roots while blossoming in fresh, new ways; so, it's worth spending a little time looking at how that dynamic has played out at JBHT.

Speaking Clearly

Leadership's influence on culture, as Kotter points out, involves setting direction, gaining alignment, and providing motivation. But how? We touched on this a bit in the previous chapter. JBHT's focus on growth and our bonus and incentive structures, for instance, are motivational in nature. And being "modal indifferent" is a strategic direction that requires alignment across business segments. Management, meanwhile, deals with the complexities of executing daily within the context of cultural norms and expectations.

Essential to both leadership and management—and therefore key to any successful culture—is a commitment to clear and consistent communication. You can't set direction, gain alignment, or provide motivation without effective communication. And when communication breaks down while managing the business, execution slides off track and culture follows.

I always tried to apply the classic K.I.S.S. formula, and I believe most leaders at JBHT do so, as well. "Keep It Simple, Stupid" was a design principle that emerged within the navy in the 1960s and makes perfect sense when it comes to communication. Leaders need to clearly articulate messages to their teams about things like mission, purpose, strategy, and expectations. If you keep things simple enough for everyone to understand, execution becomes much easier and success more likely. If you can't articulate your strategy, it's too complicated. A good message is clear and actionable. More important, it is impossible to set direction without communicating it in a simple manner. And if you teach employees to understand how the company makes money, they will set about the business of making money!

This was easier when the company was small and the number of employees were few. But with growth comes challenges, especially when thousands of the employees live and work somewhere other than where the headquarters are located. As a company grows, gaining alignment is increasingly difficult, so communication becomes even more important.

In addition to the drivers who are constantly on the road, JBHT operates terminals all across the country. The managers for our Dedicated Contract Services (DCS) work on-site with our customers. If we operate a fleet for a customer in Atlanta, our manager works from that customer's offices. In fact, of the roughly 10,000 employees who work in DCS, only about 130 are based in our corporate headquarters.

Nick Hobbs, who joined JBHT in 1984 as part of our fledgling manager training program, is now president of DCS and served previously as the segment's vice president of operations. He recognized early on the need to stress the JBHT culture with the remote employees to ensure alignment, or, as he puts it, to make sure they were "rowing on the same stroke." At the same time, he wanted them to feel the freedom to run their business units.

"In 2002, we had a low-budget meeting," Nick said. "We couldn't even afford to go to Vegas, so we went to Primm, Nevada, right on the California border, to a hole-in-the wall hotel with a conference room. I brought the regional leaders in, probably ten to twelve at the time. We went through a litany of things that were critical to us and set the standard for who we are and what we wanted to be—our core values, great service, low cost, take care of employees, and so forth."

That birthed the idea of annual operations meetings for DCS, including one in each of six regions. For the first six weekends of each year, Nick and other leaders spend two days with a different group of regional frontline managers. They talk strategy, provide updates, present awards, and cultivate the spirit of the JBHT culture. In decentralized organizations, maintaining the culture is even more important because people are making decisions independently. If they are not aligned with the culture and one another, the organization will move in too many directions.

"You're talking hundreds of people in each region," Nick said, "but it's critical that they catch the vision of where we're going and how we do things. So that's what we do."

Nick understands the importance of making sure people know the direction that has been set for the organization and of making sure people are aligned. These meetings cost more than $2 million a year, which, as John points out, is "a lot of money." But whenever he reassesses their value, he said, he always sees it as a worthy investment. Without it, the culture will not be perpetuated and the leaders can't lead.

"We feed them, we fill them up with love and stories and vision, and they go back out recharged," John said. "That's an exponential cultural impact."

At the corporate level, communication has always been stressed, initially within the core leadership team so that its members are aligned and rowing together, and then as the communications filter throughout the organization. Again, this creates an exponential impact.

"We have six or eight energized people who are then touching six or eight who are then touching six or eight," John said.

The upper leadership teams at JBHT have a history of regular meetings to discuss what's going on across the different businesses so that everyone is aligned. The success of those meetings has hinged not just on the expertise of the people involved but on their character and shared values. The leaders at the top of JBHT tend to be home-grown; that is to say, they came up through the ranks of the organization. They might have worked somewhere else for a time, but many of them have spent their entire adult lives working for JBHT and the others have worked with the company long enough to understand the culture and to earn everyone's trust and understand our values. This creates high degrees of alignment. The leaders check their egos at the door, work toward common goals, and seldom slip into petty infighting or engage in turf wars. When the leadership team operates this way, so do the managers who work for them. The values of our culture drive this outcome, which is critical for alignment. This is why culture is such an important foundation for leadership.

"We trust one another and there isn't any of what I call closet talk," Craig said. "If you have an issue with someone, you can pick up the phone and talk. The company has done a great job of not having the infighting. That doesn't mean we always agree. We have healthy discussions inside our meetings. But when we walk out, I never feel like people were backstabbing me, I never question motives, and I have confidence they are doing great things in their areas and I need to worry about my area."

Around the time Wayne returned as chairman, we instituted a weekly meeting for our top twelve executives. It began at 6:30 a.m. every Thursday, and it wasn't optional. If you were in California, you called in at 4:30 a.m. West Coast time, and you might have spent all night trying to download data over a 1990s dial-up modem. John still values those meetings today, and there are other meetings among other layers of leadership throughout the organization. These meetings can be time-consuming and their value ebbs and flows, but the risk of not having them is that leaders slip into silos and critical communication gets stifled. Even if the direction of the organization is well established in the eyes of the leaders, without this communication, it will not filter into the remainder of the organization.

"Everybody in the company works for somebody in there," Craig said. "The meetings serve as a way to get information out to about twenty people so they can tell the people who work underneath them. It's a way to keep the focus together about what we were working on. You know what other groups are working on. And it eliminates the closet talk."

Splitting Hairs

Craig remembers how the meetings made a very real difference in the direction of the company in 2006 when he and his team were exploring ways to improve their drug-testing procedures for truck drivers. There had been two serious accidents in which both drivers ended up with positive post-accident drug tests. This was frustrating, because we already performed random drug testing by taking urine samples. But Craig learned that most evidence of drugs are out of the urine within seventy-two hours, whereas evidence of drug use stays in human hair for up to ninety days. Taking a one-inch sample of hair would produce a much more accurate and fair test, so Craig brought up the idea at one of the Thursday meetings.

"Craig, you come in here every week and tell us you're short of drivers," one of the other leaders said. "Now you're going to do this test? How many drivers will this cut out?"

"I have no idea," Craig told the group. "I don't know if it will be 2 percent or 5 percent or 10 percent. But it's going to reduce our pool some."

"Let's get this right. We are short on drivers right now, and you're going come up with a test that makes our driver pool even shorter?"

"Yeah," Craig said. "We'll eliminate the ones who do drugs."

Everyone looked at each other said, "Let's do the hair testing."

We rolled out the new testing in DCS. Even with advanced warning, 14 percent of the drivers tested positive for drug use. That's dropped over the years to about 5 percent. During that first year, Craig said about 4,000 drivers who passed urine tests failed the hair testing. Since hair is not a government-approved specimen for drug testing, we continue to do the less effective urine drug tests, but we spend about $500,000 more each year to add the tougher test. We believe we save money because it reduces the number of legal settlements related to accidents involving drivers under the influence of drugs or alcohol that injure or kill other motorists. The testing also reflects our commitment to safety, which is highly valued in our culture. Craig, in fact, was our first "chief safety officer" and led the initial push to make this a priority throughout JBHT.

"When I told my wife about that title she said, 'That's great. Just what does a chief safety officer do?'" Craig said. "I told her, 'Hell if I know, but it must be important because Wayne and Kirk told me that's what I'm going to do.' They wanted me to make sure safety was on the forefront of everybody's mind. To their credit, the reason safety is so important to our culture today is because when they launched that, they stood behind it big time, every step of the way. When I held meetings, I didn't have to ask for people twice. If I did, they knew I was hot."

In other words, you can say your culture should value safety, but that value won't become ingrained in the culture unless it's fully backed by leadership (with direction, alignment, and motivation) so that it can be successfully executed by management.

Here's a real-world example: Craig recalled a trip to our Houston terminal on which he met some resistance to his safety message. He had noticed that the passenger side mirrors on many of the trucks weren't set correctly, which made it harder for the drivers to see small cars or people on that side of the trailer. He called a meeting to show drivers how to set them correctly. When the terminal manager said all the operators were busy and couldn't come in for the lesson, Craig made it clear he wasn't asking for their participation, he was insisting.

"You go get them out here now," Craig said. "I've got a plane to catch in two and a half hours, and it's not because I'm going home to cuddle with my wife next to a fire. It's because I'm going to be in California late tonight doing this same thing tomorrow morning. I'm here now and we need to talk about it. We're going to learn about safety."

Craig said he never would have been that forceful if he hadn't felt he had the support of the executive team. "I wasn't going to take no for an answer," he said. "I never doubted that they had our back when we talked about safety."

Talking about safety—in the maintenance shops, as well as on the roads—soon became part of the culture. We became very transparent about accidents—what happened, how it happened, and who was impacted. By sharing the pain and the grief that was caused by accidents, regardless of who was at fault, our employees empathized on a personal level and bought in to our commitment.

"When there's a bad accident and you get the word out," Craig said, "you can tell there's a stench or fog that comes across the company."

The commitment to safety has been put to the test several times, but perhaps never more so than one Christmas Eve when an ice storm caused several accidents between Memphis and Dallas. Craig was called anytime there was an accident, and after the third such call that night he went to the office and made the decision to shut down our fleet throughout the area of the storm. One of our customers was livid, because it meant his store wouldn't get its order on schedule. But our executive team stuck by Craig's decision as the right thing to do.

"I don't see truck numbers and alpha codes," Craig said, referencing the way equipment and drivers are tracked in computer systems. "I see moms and dads and grand moms and grand dads and sons and daughters. When you can break safety down to that, it makes a difference in your decisions. In fact, it's not just about safety. You push to get a guy or gal unloaded on time, because you know their families are counting on them having a paycheck to pay their bills. Getting them back on the road on time might make of difference of $50, but you don't blow off $50. That $50 to a driver might mean not losing their house."

The Wars for Talent

The interplay between leadership, management, and culture also has been evident in our approach to staffing. As CEO, for instance, one of the drums I beat with regularity involved the need to find and keep good drivers. "He who has the driver wins" was a battle cry in the 1990s, but it proved to be elusive. The perennial problem of attracting and retaining qualified, safe truck drivers has guided and shaped many of the strategic directions of JBHT. It slowed our growth in the mid-1980s and caused us to chase several growth vehicles that turned out to be dry holes. But it also helps make our Intermodal business such an attractive alternative to over-the-road transportation, and it partially prompted our entry into DCS and ICS.

In the 1990s, we not only wanted to attract more drivers, we wanted more experienced drivers. Research had told us that veteran drivers were involved in fewer accidents, but some of the best drivers weren't showing much interest in driving for us. So, Craig set about leading a committee to address the driver shortage. Organizing is one of the key components of management and Craig can do it well.

To better understand the challenges we faced, he and others on the committee literally went to major truck stops across America and interviewed thousands of drivers. Craig would see a driver parking his or her rig, and then he would walk out and start a conversation about J.B. Hunt Transport. He quickly learned the good and the bad.

The bad?

First of all, the drivers didn't care for JBHT's equipment. At the time, we mainly used "cab over" trucks, meaning the cab sat on top of the engine and the windshield was parallel with the very front of the cab. There were a number of advantages to these cabs, most notably that they provided better visibility for drivers, they were easier to maneuver, and they weighed less than conventional tractors. The weight difference compensated for the heavier containers we were using at the time for Intermodal. But drivers hated cab-overs because there wasn't much room in the cabs, which are literally a driver's home-away-from-home during a long trip.

"I'm not laying on my back to put on my pants for any man," the drivers would say.

The drivers also didn't like sitting so close to the front of the tractor.

"You know who arrives first at the scene of an accident that involves a cab-over?" the drivers would ask rhetorically. "Me. The truck driver. I'll be the first one there because I'm right up against the glass."

Another negative was that we had restricted our trucks to 59 miles per hour in an effort to save on fuel costs. In hindsight, this was mostly a marketing problem—59 just sounded so dang slow. Here's where we could have borrowed from the approach used by retailers who price items at just under the dollar—$6.99 instead of $7, for instance. It's the perception. We easily could have gone with 60 mph instead of 59. It wouldn't have cost that much more on our fuel bills, and we could have avoided the negative perception.

The other two biggest negatives were that some drivers didn't want to wear a uniform or keep a professional look and that they didn't like that they weren't allowed to be permanently assigned to a specific truck. Instead, they were "slip-seated" into a JBHT truck. Most drivers went home when they took time off, and they took their tractor with them until it was time for the next run. When our drivers took time off, we slipped another driver into that seat and the truck kept rolling so we could maximize the use of equipment.

We could make changes to address some of these issues. We eventually went to conventional cab tractors, for instance. But that took time. On other points, we weren't so willing to budge, either for economic reasons (like with slip-seating) or for the health of the culture (like with the commitment to a professional look).

At the end of the interviews, Craig asked the hard question: *How much would we have to pay you to make all those negatives worth it?* When they analyzed the answers, they determined it would take a 33 percent pay hike. And with much trepidation, that's what we did.

We knew that type of increase would help us attract more veteran drivers, so one of the ways we offset the cost was by closing our driving schools. And, as I noted earlier, we believed placing a bigger emphasis on safety would save money by reducing payouts from lawsuits.

36 | PURPLE ON THE INSIDE

"There are people today who will tell you the pay increase didn't work and people who will tell you it worked," Craig said. "I say it worked. Turnover went down overnight. People say pay doesn't matter on turnover. They're totally wrong. The better you treat someone, the less premium you have to pay. But pay does matter. It isn't the only thing. You can treat somebody so bad that it doesn't matter what you pay them. But pay does matter. We cut turnover in half."

It's difficult to compare driver turnover rates in the transportation industry, because different companies calculate it differently. Some, for instance, don't count drivers who leave within ninety days of being hired. But it's not uncommon for driver turnover in truckload to be more than 100 percent a year.

Ultimately, Craig's management talent allowed him to organize the research to determine what needed to be done to correct the problem. He was aligned with the direction of the company because he was deeply immersed in a culture with clear values and he knew he was empowered to move forward with the research. The leadership team set the direction—get great drivers—but the values showed that it couldn't be done by sacrificing quality standards in driver selection. Everyone was aligned because the direction was communicated clearly, simply, and frequently. All of this was confirmed and the values even more established in the culture when the leadership team made the decision to implement the recommendations. This was a resounding affirmation of the values and direction given the magnitude of the expense.

Taking Charge

All too often, today's leaders view "culture" as something they should create to appease the masses, and this can result in some unhealthy outcomes. There's nothing wrong with collaborating with employees. As I said at the start of this chapter, one-man shows are for carnivals or hot dog stands, not corporate America. We value a collaborative culture. At the same time, leaders hold their positions for a reason, and there are times when we need to take a strong stand. Thomas Jefferson put it this way: "In matters of style, swim with the current; in matters of principle, stand like a rock." Employees need and want leaders who will take charge, and strong leadership, I believe, has been a vital part of the JBHT culture.

John remembers learning this lesson around the time we lost our biggest customer in DCS and effectively had to park 20 percent of that segment's fleet. It was a humbling event, John says, because up to that point he had experienced nothing but rock-star success as the leader of DCS. He had to do some self-evaluation. But he also had to reset the organization and challenge his team.

"There was a time when I was very philosophical about management in a trouble zone, and I thought a touchy-feely approach would work," John said. "So, I wrote a letter to my leadership team in DCS. It said something like, 'Dear Partner. Imagine we'd just been hired as a new management team to come in and fix this company. And blah, blah, blah.' Real soft, feel-good stuff. And I asked them to bring their ideas. No sacred cows, I told them. We needed to lean up."

John's team responded by having a retreat and coming back with equally soft recommendations. They told him he should fire his assistant, because that was overhead we didn't need, and that he should stop flying on the company airplane, because that sent the wrong message.

"It was not what I was looking for," John said.

He brought the letter to me in search of advice. I'll let him describe what happened.

"Kirk had a red pen and he completely filleted that letter," he said. "The first thing he marked out was *partner*. He said, 'These people are not your partners. They are not of equal weight to you. You are confusing people. This is soft. You are in trouble right now. Take decisive action.' I went back and constructed a list of what they all were going to go do based on my judgment of what was wrong in their areas. I called them in one by one and said, 'This is what you're going to do and this is when you're going to have it done. And if you don't want to do that, tender your resignation. I am not going down like this. We can fix this. But you're going to do it my way.' I later found out that's exactly what they wanted. They wanted me to lead them. They wanted me to give them direction. Once they found some purpose in that direction, they were able to take ownership of it."

Here's the moral of that story in leadership: We have to set a clear expectation. We have to tell people exactly what we want them to go do. We don't have to tell them how. But we have to tell them exactly where the finish line is, exactly where the goal post is. Precisely. Crystal clear expectations are required.

That strength in leadership comes with balance. One of John's demands on his team was that they meet with him weekly for updates. "I'm not going to do that," one of them said. "You're right about everything else, but I'm not going to meet with you every week. I'm a grown-ass man."

John was wise enough to back off that demand.

"That taught me there is a place where you can push too far," he said. "You have to get to that edge and then slow down."

That's precisely how leadership and management interact to cultivate a vibrant culture—by developing the ability to find that balance.

"This is hugely a team sport," John said. "There is no way to win this by yourself. Sometimes it takes direction. Sometimes I have to challenge them. Sometimes I have to tough-love them. Sometimes I hug their necks. Sometimes I back off and leave them alone. But by myself, there's no way. There's no way one person can get this done."

CHAPTER 4

Feeding the Funnel

Anyone can fill a bucket.... It takes focus to feed the funnel.
—Next Marketing

T he American Trucking Association held its national convention in Chicago in the fall of 1989. This provided the perfect opportunity for a face-to-face meeting that would change the course of J.B. Hunt and dramatically reshape the freight transportation industry.

It started with a phone call from a consultant with McKinsey & Company. We had met a few years earlier when he was doing some research for Cummins Engine Company. Back then, he was seeking my opinion on an idea the diesel engine company was considering. Now he was working on a project for the Santa Fe Railway, and he wasn't just looking for an opinion—he was gauging our interest in a partnership in the railroad's intermodal business.

Intermodal transportation has been around for centuries. It simply means that you are moving freight with more than one mode. In the eighteenth century, that meant a box was loaded onto a horse-drawn wagon, then transferred to a boat for a trip up or down a river, and then loaded onto a horse-drawn wagon and taken to its final destination.

As it has evolved, the long-haul portions are handled mainly by ships and railroad, while the drayage—the short distances—are handled by trucks. The Santa Fe, like other railroads, hauled freight, but they didn't have anything to do with the drayage and they had very few direct relationships with customers. Most of their freight business was through third-party brokers, so the Santa Fe wanted to grow its intermodal business by partnering with a motor carrier.

"They aren't looking to acquire a trucking company, but they really would like to partner with one," the consultant told me. "Would you guys be interested?"

"As a matter of fact," I said, "I think we might. That sounds very intriguing."

The railroad and trucking industries have a long and mostly adversarial relationship. Early on, the railroads actually pushed the U.S. government for better roads to make it easier for trucks to move freight to and from the railyards. As the roadways across America improved, however, trucking companies began competing with the railroaders, not complementing them. For decades, railroads took every opportunity available to lobby Congress for anti-truck bills. Deregulation in 1980 only increased their fears and concerns that over-the-road trucks would cut into their business. Truckers, meanwhile, wanted changes that benefited them, not rail. We wanted trailers with more cubic capacity, for instance, and we wanted to haul heavier loads. The industries were antagonistic, to say the least.

We were always looking for new opportunities, however, and the timing of this proposal was perfect. Several other trucking companies had gone public since deregulation, and by the late 1980s there was a lot of capitalized competition in the market. Our truckload segment was depending more and more on shorter lengths of haul, which meant we had to deal with more customers and freight to drive the same revenues and utilization as longer hauls. So, when I approached J.B. about the idea of partnering with a railroad, he was just as open to it as me.

The consultant arranged for our leadership team to meet at our headquarters with Santa Fe president Mike Haverty and some of his executive officers. Haverty explained that he was riding on one of his intermodal trains when he became fixated on the trucks driving along the interstate that ran parallel to the rails. "What's wrong with this picture?" he asked himself. He saw all these trucks on the road, each with one driver, one power unit (the tractor), and one trailer. Meanwhile, his trains used one or two power units up front, needed three workers to drive it, and hauled 250 trailers.

"Somehow this doesn't make economic sense," he said. "I need to find somebody who knows how to load those trailers and make the pickups and deliveries with a tractor in an efficient way."

J.B. Hunt Transport fit the bill.

"He thought J.B. Hunt and its abilities with trucks, know-how, customer base, and reputation for high-end service could help him change the model for intermodal in the rail industry," said Paul Bergant. "If he'd made that pitch to any other trucker in the world at that time, they'd have said, 'Thank you, but no thank you' and sent him back to Chicago. For us, a light bulb went on. We talked about it. We knew our model was going to be under some strain. We had to do something to change or the outcome would be stagnation."

The Santa Fe's headquarters were in Chicago, just a few blocks from where the ATA would hold its convention later that year. So, we met again with the Santa Fe folks while we were in town, and they suggested that we ride with them on one of their trains from Chicago to Kansas City rather than flying home after the convention. Most trains at the time went through what were known as "hump yards," where they would switch cars from one train to another in a process that bumped the cars when they were hooked together. Freight sometimes was damaged in the process, which was one reason shippers were leery of moving freight on trains. The train trip not only would give us more time to talk, but it also would allow us to experience the journey the freight would make. The Santa Fe didn't use hump yards, Haverty told us when he pitched the idea of the train trip. "Ours is a smooth ride," he said.

A few days later we boarded the "business car" on their train, and off we all went. We really hit it off, and the more we learned, the more we liked. Haverty, unlike J.B., was college educated, but the two icons had plenty in common. They were big guys, visionary in their thinking, and reared on timeless values like hard work. J.B. was born in rural Heber Springs, Arkansas, and grew up during the Great Depression. Haverty, about twenty years younger than J.B., was a fourth-generation railroader who began his career as a brakeman and worked his way up. The two men weren't cut from the exact same cloth, but it was difficult to tell their visionary threads apart. As the train rolled down the tracks, Haverty and J.B. shook hands and the deal was sealed.

"J.B. walked over to me and said, 'Haverty, we've got a deal,'" Haverty told the *Arkansas Democrat-Gazette* in a 2016 interview. "I said, 'What's the deal?' He said, 'I don't know, but we're going to do it.'"[1]

"Those two being who they were," Paul pointed out, "a handshake was as good as anything."

Andy Petery, an analyst at Morgan Stanley who had been following the railroad industry and who would follow J.B. Hunt Transport for years, points out that this was a turning point for the railroad and JBHT.

"J.B. Hunt, the man and the company, recognized that the future was in

---

1. Emma N. Hurt, "Hunt Bound for Hall of Fame," *Arkansas Democrat-Gazette*, September 25, 2016.

partnering with the enemy, so to speak," Andy told us. "The enemy was the railroad. If they did it successfully, they would not only enable the railroad to compete in the trucking environment, which was 75 percent of the freight business, but J.B. Hunt the company would also expand its growth prospects by using the railroads as partners and entering markets they couldn't possibly do on their own."

After the train ride, leaders from both entities scrambled to work out the details.

"We started the process literally with a clean sheet of paper," said Paul, who led the JBHT team and would become president of our Intermodal segment. "Our models had to change, and quickly. Change did not happen in the railroad industry in days, months, or even years. We said, 'That's not going to work.' And over the next few months, it was the darndest thing you ever saw. We hardly ever ran into a road block that we didn't get over in a day or two."

By December, we had publicly announced a first-of-its-kind "strategic alliance." We called it Quantum and began with 150 trailers branded with that name. We dealt with customers, marketed the service, and priced it. The Santa Fe had input on the price, of course, but they were primarily responsible for moving the freight over the rails. Their costs were fixed, but ours fluctuated depending on the distance of the dray—how far we drove the freight to get it on the train at one end and to get it to the final destination on the other. So, we came up with a matrix for splitting the revenues.

All of this required significant changes for both us and the Santa Fe, but we worked them out over the course of time.

"They had to change the way they operated their intermodal terminals," Paul said. "We wanted to be on the terminal, not fifteen-to-twenty miles away. We needed our own gate to go in and out. They had to go through their well cars and modify every one of them for the containers we were building so they would sit down in them. On and on it went. So, there were fundamental changes."

JBHT had to make adjustments, as well.

"We took some of the best freight in our network and took it off trucks and put it on the railroads," Paul said. "Then we had to sell our customers on the fact that this brand of intermodal was totally different than they had tried in the past or heard about. That was no easy change in thought. But we stuck with it and the railroad worked with us when we went to customers. Once they

tried it, they found this thing was pretty darn good. It was a reliable s
an opportunity to save money because of the efficiencies of it."

It didn't take us long to discover that we'd hit on something big. In fact, we
quickly moved beyond the Quantum trailers and made our entire fleet—about
10,000 trailers—available for Intermodal. This gave shippers more options
and increased our efficiencies. After a year, Intermodal was producing $30 mil-
lion in revenue. Before long, we added agreements with Burlington Northern
for routes to the Pacific Northwest and with Con-Rail for routes to the East
Coast. Those original deals have survived multiple mergers within the railroad
industry, and today we're the biggest provider of intermodal services in North
America. It's the largest revenue segment in our company, and, I might add, it
was good for the railroad industry, too.

"I think the stock of Santa Fe the day they shook hands was relatively low,"
Paul pointed out. "Four or five years later when they merged with Burlington
Northern, it was way up. Everybody won. The motor carrier, the railroads, and
the customer. It changed the model of an industry."

This segment of our business represents something more than just a mon-
umental success story—although it certainly is that. It also represents an approach to business that made J.B. Hunt Transport prosperous from the beginning and still factors into our growth and long-term success.

An Eye for Opportunity

J.B. Hunt began in the rice-hull business because he saw an opportunity. The
company then expanded to trucking because he saw opportunities there. In
fact, J.B. was the classic entrepreneur, a leader who saw opportunities nearly
everywhere he looked. Frankly, it could drive the rest of us crazy.

"He was a dreamer," Craig Harper told us. "Thank goodness he had Mrs.
Hunt and Kirk Thompson and Wayne Garrison to keep those dreams in check,
but at the same time allow some of them to prove to be fantastic businesses."

We were "feeding the funnel" with all these new business ideas. We didn't
call it that; in fact, our strategy wasn't based on any particular business theory,
just common sense. We were founded by an entrepreneur who seldom met
a new business idea he didn't like. His passion to try new things required a
counterbalance, which his wife and the rest of the leadership team provided.

In retrospect, from a business economics perspective, you could say that "options pricing theory" and "decision theory" were playing out even though we didn't consciously embrace those ideas from a business theory perspective. Every good business needs new ideas that allow it to keep up with, or, better yet, stay ahead of the times. Most businesses, however, focus on the task at hand—often until it's too late. Newspaper companies focused on printing news on paper until the Internet forced them to see the world differently. Taxi companies focused on their historic model and were caught off guard by new players like Uber and Lyft. Keeping the funnel full is the key to creative destruction (which we'll discuss more in the next chapter), because a full funnel presents options that allow a company to innovate.

In the investment world, some traders specialize in buying options. They identify stocks they believe will go up faster and higher than the market predicts. Rather than buying those stocks, however, they buy call options on those stocks. For a much smaller investment, they purchase the call option to buy the stock at a locked-in price, known as the strike price. If and when the stock price rises, the investor can buy at the lower, locked-in rate and immediately sell at the current (higher) market value. On the other hand, if the price stays the same or drops, the investor is only out the amount spent on the option. They could have lost more if they had bought the underlying stock. J.B. Hunt Transport has always kept its options side alive by investing in new ideas without going all in right away. Some of them, like Intermodal, have paid off with huge returns, while others provided more modest returns or were eventually shut down or sold off.

In the late 1980s and early 1990s, we looked for anything that might lessen our dependence on truckload trucking. As mentioned earlier, we eventually had to pull back and focus on the ideas we saw as potential purple cows. But it's unlikely we would have found those game-changers had we not fed the funnel with so many options. We expanded into the flatbed and short-haul business, created a first-of-its-kind partnership that took us into Mexico with Hunt de Mexico, and launched a special commodities segment that primarily hauled hazardous waste materials. And, we partnered with the Santa Fe on intermodal. This partnership provided the option of going all-in if the intermodal business worked out. If it had not worked out, we were only out the amount we spent developing and executing the partnership.

Most trucking companies viewed intermodal as too risky, even after we had proved its success. I'll share a quick story to illustrate the mindset of most leaders in the trucking industry when it came to intermodal.

The Arkansas Trucking Association once hosted a panel discussion titled something along the lines of "Mistakes I've Made in Trucking." When they asked me to be a panelist, I wondered how much time I'd get to talk, because I'd need all I could get to cover all my mistakes! The thing is, I don't even remember the big mistake I talked about whenever it was my turn to share. But I vividly remember the response it drew from Bob Weaver, who at the time was CEO of PAM Transportation Services.

"I thought you were going to say buying all those containers," he said.

I might have, except for one thing: That wasn't a mistake. In fact, "buying all of those containers," as he put it, was instrumental to the growth of Intermodal. While the rest of the trucking industry was trying to decide if it really made sense to partner with a competitor in a deal that took business away from over-the-road trucking, we invested in customized containers and chassis that gave us a competitive edge. We spent millions on new fifty-three-foot containers that could carry the same amount of freight as a fifty-three-foot trailer and still hold up to the loading and unloading process that came with intermodal. Unlike with our normal truckload trailers, we could double-stack the containers in well cars, with one sitting down in the well and the other locked on top. That allowed us to haul twice as much freight per rail car. And the chassis we built to carry those containers were unique, so no one else could use them.

Why did we invest so much in Intermodal? We saw the potential it held over all the other business opportunities we were considering. Decision theory requires consideration of the potential gains and losses while factoring in the risks. We had to consider what worked well and what didn't, and then invest where it made the most sense for the overall future of the business.

The initial investment in Intermodal wasn't as risky as many thought. At the time, we didn't run many truck teams from Chicago to California, so partnering with the railroad on this lane was a lower risk, while still leaving options to partner on other lanes. Decision theory makes it clear that for a given set of costs and benefits, selecting alternatives with lower down-side risk, other things being equal, increases the expected payoff. In fact, it added to our business without requiring us to hire more long-haul drivers at a time when drivers were in high demand. As we began to see positive returns, it made sense to expand beyond Quantum and use our entire fleet, then to expand to other parts of the country, and then to invest in the specialized containers and chassis. Meanwhile, we were letting go of other opportunities in our funnel because they weren't providing the same expected returns (chopping wood, as we've previously mentioned). The biggest beneficiary of our early entry into intermodal services was our customer base. We could now offer long-distance freight service at a reduced cost.

This approach allowed us to identify and focus on Intermodal, but also to explore options that led to Dedicated Contract Service (DCS), where we manage logistics for a shipper's private fleet, and Integrated Capacity Solutions (ICS), where we operate as a sophisticated broker. It's an approach that remains a high priority for the future.

Stuart Scott, whose background includes positions at GE and Microsoft prior to joining J.B. Hunt Transport in 2016 as chief information officer, points out that JBHT is a logistics company with extensive information capabilities that is turning itself into an information company with logistics capacities. To discover where that transformation will take the company, JBHT will continue to feed the funnel with innovative ideas and focus on the ones that work best for our customers and shareholders.

CHAPTER 5

Tipping Your CAPs

Thrifty, hardworking, unemotional, they tipped their hats to no one.
— *Longman Dictionary of Contemporary English*

O ne of the distinguishing marks of a genuine purple cow business segment is that it's extremely difficult — if not impossible — to replicate.
If it weren't, competitors would mirror your successes and you would
no longer have a competitive advantage.

Creating barriers to entry that make it difficult for the competition to follow
your roadmap of success is the subject of countless business books. Those barriers have proven important in JBHT's success, but we've come up with a term
that represents how the company established, maintained, and even overcame
competitive advantages. We call it Controlled Access Points, or CAPs.

One leadership mantra at J.B. Hunt Transport is to "focus on what you can
control." This is a solutions-oriented mindset for dealing with specific problems, but it's also the best way to understand where you should focus from a
strategic perspective. Our job is to deliver results, so we believe in eliminating
the "but for's" from our vocabulary. . . . "but for the weather, we would have
been on time" . . . "but for the price of fuel, we would have made more money."
Excuses don't solve problems, so don't worry about the stuff you can't control.
And above all, don't feed problems while starving opportunities.

Controlled Access Points (CAPs) are a way of feeding the opportunities.

To understand what we mean by CAPs, think about the interstate highway
system, which is essentially a network of roads with Controlled Access Points.
The same design is employed with toll roads, railroad yards, shipping harbors,
and airports. There are designated places where you can enter and exit. Access
is controlled. In business, there are strategic levers that leaders should identify and manipulate to overcome, create, or sustain competitive advantages.
Most companies ignore this approach, largely because they're too focused on

day-to-day operations. They are busy grooming that brown cow. We haven't always managed these opportunities as well as we could have at JBHT, but we frequently identified CAPs and used them in our favor to change the game.

CAPs are evident in all four of JBHT's primary business segments, and they are big reasons why the company was able to turn three of those into purple cows. But perhaps the most surprising example of the impact of CAPs took place in truckload trucking, which isn't purple but is foundational to the history and the future of J.B. Hunt Transport.

In the 1950s, J.B. worked as a truck driver for Superior Forwarding Company, mainly driving a route between Little Rock and St. Louis. He learned the trucking business from the inside of the cab out. So, in 1969, with his rice-hull business doing well financially, he invested in five used trucks and seven used trailers, and the company began a side business hauling poultry.

At the time, however, there were significant barriers to entry into the truckload business. Barriers to entry can come in many forms—high startup costs, limited market size, or, as was the case in trucking, governmental regulations. The Motor Carrier Act of 1935 required truckers to get a "certificate of public convenience and necessity"—more commonly known as "authorities"—from the Interstate Commerce Commission (ICC). Established companies were grandfathered in and granted "permanent authorities." They essentially were given first right of refusal for hauling freight, so they were able to keep their rates high and didn't have to worry much about competition from upstarts like J.B. Hunt.

If you weren't one of the legacy carriers—like Jones Truck Lines, Yellow Freight, or Roadway Express—then you had to convince a shipper to support your efforts to gain their business. Next you had to apply for authority from the ICC. For instance, if Mobile Chemical agreed to hire you to haul egg cartons from Temple, Texas, to delivery points in five states, you'd file an application with the ICC, it would be published in the *Federal Register*, and a comment period would commence during which the legacy carriers would oppose your application for various reasons, most which were code for, "We don't want more competition." As you might imagine, we had to fight tooth and nail to get new authorities that were the key to growing the trucking business.

In the early days, Cy Cypert was our ICC practitioner. He wasn't an attorney, but he was licensed to argue our cases before the ICC. He was a very funny, very smart cat who worked for us until he retired. Cy knew all the objections the legacy companies would raise in their attempts to keep us from getting new business, and he usually had a clever retort for each one. One example in particular has always stuck with me.

Jones Truck Lines (JTL), which was based not far from us in Springdale, Arkansas, was one of the bigger legacy trucking companies in the country, with a history dating back to 1918. JTL once filed a brief against us based on the fact that we operated warehouses. Indeed, we had warehousing at the time, but it didn't make a lot of money and it had no bearing on the route we wanted. Nevertheless, the brief filed by JTL made a comment that said something like, "Whether or not J.B. Hunt will offer discounted or free warehousing to gain the transportation business, who can say?" In his rebuttal, Cy said, "If you have the facts, pound the facts. If you have the law, pound the law. If you have neither, pound the table." We all thought it was a classic line, although our friends at JTL weren't so amused. I don't recall if we won that case, but I've never forgotten that phrase and I've used it many times over the years.

When Cy retired, we started using a transportation ICC law firm in Chicago named Singer and Sullivan. Paul Bergant was a staff attorney at the firm and traveled extensively with Paul Maestri, our general manager, which gave him an inside view of our company. Because Paul (Bergant) also worked with some of our competitors, he could see the difference between how we did things and where we were going. So, when we offered him a position with JBHT in 1978, he jumped at the opportunity.

"My last day at the office in Chicago, we went to Wrigley Field for a going-away party," Paul recalled. "And afterward we were at some pub and one of the guys said, 'I know you're looking forward to Arkansas, and that's a great company. But what if that doesn't work out?' To this day, I still haven't answered that question."

Paul, who spent thirty-three years with JBHT before retiring in 2011, had no Plan B because he realized the winds of deregulation were blowing and that we were well positioned to fill our sails.

"The whole strategy and culture was different than other companies that were out there that had been around a long time and, in many cases, were more successful," Paul said. "Hunt had ideas that gave it the opportunity to trump those competitors—things that the industry takes for granted today, like the uniformity of the tractors and trailers."

Those were among the levers we could control when Paul joined our team, but it took a few years before they paid off because the regulated industry favored the legacy carriers. We occasionally won the rights to authorities from the ICC. Otherwise, our trucking segment relied largely on "trip leases," which was essentially subcontracting with a legacy carrier, or hauling "exempt commodities," which were mainly agricultural products that weren't bound by ICC regulations.

Balance is key in trucking. If you haul something to Chicago, you need something to haul out of Chicago so you don't burn a lot of miles with an empty trailer. Trip leases and exempt commodities helped us achieve balance, but neither of them made much money. The rates for exempt commodities were notoriously cheap, and trip leases were arranged either by the legacy companies (who controlled how much we were paid) or brokers (who were notoriously slow to pay). Trip leases also were a hassle because we had to put the other company's signs on our trucks.

"The first ten years of the trucking company were really a struggle," Johnelle said. "Everything we touched didn't turn to gold, and everything we did didn't work, but we always tried to make it work. . . . We knew if it all failed we could go back to where we were and be happy. I think that's the secret—don't be afraid. Because if you're afraid of losing, you'll never make it."[1]

In light of all these barriers and struggles, the outside accountants often encouraged the Hunts to get out of the trucking business. We had several morning meetings where cash flow was a major topic as we decided who to pay first and which obligations we could put off for another day, week, or month.

"That got kind of wearisome," Paul said. "I've heard Mr. Hunt tell this story, but one morning, probably around 1980, we had a meeting and somebody said something along the lines that maybe we should think about bankruptcy. There was just silence and the meeting just broke up and it was never brought up again. The next day, everybody just came back to work. We just rolled our sleeves up and kept at it. It wasn't long after that that we started to catch our stride, to the point that in 1983 we went public.

"I imagine every small business experiences that. It wears you down because you wonder if you're ever going to get out of that hole and have the breathing room to do what you want. But that meeting showed the resolve and the faith. It was a small company, but there were a lot of people who believed

---

1. Emma Hurt, "J.B. Hunt to Be Bestowed Hall of Fame Seat," *Arkansas Democrat-Gazette*, September 25, 2016.

in it. What happens if it doesn't work out? Well, go to work and work harder. We knew we were building something, we just hadn't gotten the momentum yet to sustain it."

When the environment began to change in the late 1970s, we were perfectly positioned to take advantage of the Controlled Access Points—but only because we didn't give up when times looked bleak. First, the ICC began easing up on the nonlegacy carriers. It was, in effect, administratively deregulating. Then the Motor Carrier Act of 1980 made deregulation official and opened the doors for a free-for-all competition. Now there were new access points within our control. We could negotiate directly with shippers and everything was fair game. It opened up a whole new world. We were able to exert our ability to create balance, woo the customer, give good service, and win business based on merits rather than the government dictating who got to control what.

There were winners and losers in deregulation. The losers tended to be the ones who had enjoyed government protection and maybe had gotten a little fat and happy. They had the barriers that protected them. When that went away, they weren't as agile. They didn't adjust. Rather than finding new access points to control, they let the market and the competition control them. Some of the legacy carriers weren't willing to compete. Competition drove down prices, so some of them just shut down the truckload part of their business or sold it off. Others tried to compete and failed because they weren't accustomed to operating efficiently. With the barriers to entry removed, many new carriers emerged, but most of them failed or never grew to any significant size.

For JBHT, the battles to survive in a highly regulated industry prepared us to compete in trucking when the access points changed and set the stage for us to develop the other very profitable segments of our business. You learn a whole lot more from struggles in the valley than you do on the mountaintop. The struggles we had before deregulation toughened us and made us appreciate the idea that we had to work hard and get our hands dirty to make success happen. The disadvantages in those regulated years helped mold us. In fact, I think the trucking companies that did well in deregulation were the ones that persisted through times of intense struggle. We still had to do it right in terms of costs, treating employees and drivers right, and customer service. That hurdle of convincing the government to grant us the business, however, was no longer there. Now it was a matter of execution on fundamentals.

It wasn't just that the major barrier had been removed. Game plans are important. Qualified and creative team members are critical. But it's execution that stirs the soup. You can have the greatest players and an ironclad strategy, but execution is of paramount importance. Without execution, your cow is likely to stay brown. We also were able to pull other strategic levers that worked in our favor. By focusing on things we could control, we had grown efficient and skilled in several important areas. In effect, we were able to race onto the highway because we had the right blend of moxie, marketing, execution, and innovation that all combined during a good economy and just as the market went from closed to free.

Despite our struggles in the trucking segment, and partly because of them, we were constantly looking for competitive advantages. We were pioneers, as mentioned earlier, in the practice of "slip seating" trucks. It was a much more efficient and effective use of equipment. The Less-Than-Truckload (LTL) companies already did this, but it was uncommon in the truckload business.

We also were quick to move from forty-foot trailers to forty-eight-foot trailers and then to fifty-three-foot trailers as soon as the regulations allowed. We were growing our fleet as the regulations were changing, so upgrading was part of our natural growth. It allowed us to offer more cubic feet of space for the same rate. And because we regulated the maximum speed for our trucks and used new equipment, our fuel efficiency and maintenance costs were much better than many other carriers.

Paul became our head of marketing in the post-deregulation era (he later would run our Intermodal business). He had dealt with customers during the tougher times, so he had the relationships that helped grow the business during the go-go years that led to our public offering in 1983.

One of Paul's big wins came just before deregulation when he secured a contract with Wal-Mart. The retailer, which is based in Bentonville, Arkansas, just a few miles north of our headquarters, mainly used the legacy carriers; in particular, Jones Truck Line in nearby Springdale, Arkansas.

"Our offices were on the old Highway 71 back then," Paul remembered. "Jones was a big carrier that had been around forever, and their equipment would go by our office every day headed for Bentonville—hundreds of them every day."

Wal-Mart, which was founded in 1962 and went public in 1970, was growing like crazy in the 1970s, so Paul began cautiously approaching people there and building relationships. Then one day he got a call saying Wal-Mart had decided to support JBHT for authority to carry products to their expanding network of distribution centers.

"I'll never forget coming back with that signed document," Paul said. "It was like time stopped for a minute. It was like our ship finally had a chance to launch and have a real opportunity to catch some momentum. That was a major breakthrough in terms of acceptance."

We still didn't do a ton of business with Wal-Mart, but that contract opened a door just as deregulation was ending. Because we were picking up freight to deliver to Wal-Mart, we were developing new relationships with major manufacturers around the country like Ralston Purina, Procter & Gamble, and the plastics segment of Mobil Oil. We soon won contracts that had nothing to do with Wal-Mart. But, as Paul put it, the Wal-Mart deal was "a key jumpstart to open the national customer book, and it gave us an opportunity to try to grow the way we wanted."

In 1977, our revenue was $6.5 million with earnings of $333,214, and we employed 127 people. By 1983, the year we went public and three years into deregulation, our revenue had grown to $63 million, our earnings to $8.4 million, and our team to more than 1,000 people. Our fleet also had grown from fewer than 90 trucks and fewer than 120 trailers to 550 trucks and more than 1,000 trailers. It was just the beginning, of course, but it wouldn't have happened if we hadn't identified those CAPs and leveraged them to position us for success.

CAPS for Our Purple Cows

Controlled Access Points also played a key role in the growth of Intermodal, Dedicated Contract Services (DCS), and Integrated Capacity Solutions (ICS).

As discussed earlier, we were the first trucking company to partner with a major railroad to jointly offer intermodal transportation, which, for us, is simply moving a trailer or container over long distances by train and attaching it to a truck for the short-haul or pick-up and delivery part of its journey.

Rail and trucking have historically been competing industries, so most intermodal business had been arranged by brokers. But our joint venture with the Santa Fe Railway in 1989 was a game-changer. The railroads needed brokers because the brokers had relationships with shippers. We already had strong relationships with truckload shippers, so we were positioned to market and sell intermodal in partnership with a rail carrier. That's one reason that led the Santa Fe Railway to approach us with the idea of a joint partnership in intermodal. We effectively offered shippers an option that cut out the middlemen.

The early financial success of the joint intermodal venture convinced us to invest and expand that business while others were still looking at it as a risky endeavor between two competitors that everyone else believed wouldn't be able to get along. But we added partnerships with other railroads to serve more of the country, invested in customized containers and chassis, and locked in agreements that gave us priority over other carriers with the loading and unloading of our cargo and with our entry and exit of the railyards, among other things.

There are fixed costs associated with switching to rail and back, but the cost per ton mile is much lower on rail. So, for intermodal to be efficient, you need relatively long moves to make up for the fixed cost associated with switching. In general, the minimum distance needed to make intermodal competitive decreases based on a combination of factors—higher truckload rates, lower rail rates, higher fuel prices, and lower fixed costs associated with switching modes. We developed more experience than any other carrier with full-load intermodal, hence our fixed costs associated with switching between modes steadily decreased, which created a competitive advantage. Costs have decreased for three main reasons: (1) we created assets for this purpose, (2) we created business processes for this purpose, including the all-important achievement of balanced traffic lanes and reduction of empty legs, and (3) we have traveled the learning/experience curve. The lengths-of-haul where intermodal is the best option continues to contract as drivers become more and more scarce, highways become more congested, truck rates increase due to higher costs, and shippers increasingly focus on reducing greenhouse gas emissions. Intermodal is far friendlier to the environment due to its much lower carbon footprint.

Our biggest competition in intermodal remains brokers. These companies don't own much in the way of physical assets. They simply work as a go-between by arranging for a trucker to haul the freight to and from the railroad and arranging for the railroad to handle the long-distance haul. On the other hand, we have the assets. We use company drivers for 90 percent of our trucks, which helps ensure consistent service. And we have dedicated ingress and egress at the railyards, meaning we have our own gates with our own inspection stations to get in and out of yards more quickly. The reduction in fixed cost associated with intermodal allows us to economically provide shorter hauls through intermodal than our competitors.

Very few truckload companies have followed us into the intermodal business, in part because it takes experience, customer acceptance, unique business processes, density, scale and scope, and technology. The unique business processes, it turns out, are very difficult to emulate. In addition, nobody wants to make the investment. We've got more than 92,000 containers, plus chassis, so that alone represents more than $2 billion. That's more than a mouthful for anybody else. Plus, we have the trucks for the pickup and delivery. It's a big investment, and it is a CAP that we control. Then, using all of these effectively and efficiently is a CAP in our control, because it takes experience, customer acceptance, unique business processes, and technology.

We have so much business, so many boxes, so much money invested, do such a good job, and have such a good reputation with customers that, for the most part, we're the preferred provider of intermodal. And we have lower costs because of it. All of these things together are the embodiment of the purple cow we have in intermodal. It's a business that's not easily duplicated.

But the thing that really separated us from everyone else who tried intermodal was that we really bought into it. Our view was that we should give the shipper what they need. If we got a truckload and we knew it would be better for the shipper to put it on intermodal, we didn't hold on tightly and say, "Let's don't do that because that might hurt our trucking business." We did—and still do—whatever makes the most sense for the customer. And in the end, everyone wins.

This was the attitude that led us to launch our ICS segment. ICS is, by definition, a brokerage firm, and it might seem like there are very few CAPs for a brokerage firm. But when that firm is part of a larger organization like J.B. Hunt Transport, it can provide services, expertise, and options that other firms can't.

The key to success with ICS is connecting shippers with transportation capacity in ways that drives value to shippers. This is an information and coordination challenge, so sophisticated information systems are the key to success. We've developed information systems that utilize shipper data and carrier data, that are user friendly to shippers and carriers, and that help customers make better decisions more quickly. And we're able to track performance, which is critical to market dominance—but also a huge and ongoing investment. That investment becomes a barrier to entry for others trying to enter the market. In the past, all you needed to broker freight was a phone. Now you need big data, data scientists, and optimization. These were access points we've been able to control to raise higher barriers to entry and higher profitability, both for us and for the shippers who use our systems.

DCS is another segment where at first glance it might seem like other carriers could replicate anything we do well and, thereby, threaten our market share. But we've found CAPs in this segment, as well.

DCS allows shippers to outsource their freight services rather than owning and managing a fleet. Since we are highly profitable, publicly traded, and have a great reputation and financial strength, we can bring the capital to develop or convert private fleets in ways that our competitors cannot. For instance, David Mee, our CFO, was recognized in 2016 as one of the best chief financial officers in the nation by *Institutional Investor Magazine*, which named him to its 2017 All-America Executive Team. Being the best in the industry at managing and deploying capital provides a competitive advantage in winning new fleet business. We also take their liability and workers compensation risks away, and we bring expertise on engineering, design, and proprietary processes and technologies.

The more private fleets we take over, the better we get at working with shippers to deliver value. And our overall experience in the transportation services industry also provides a significant advantage. It allows us to excel in areas where we face the stiffest competition, but to branch out and take on challenges others shy away from. For most of our competitors, dedicated service means offering what we call fifty-three-foot drop-and-hook service from a distribution center to a store. In other words, they take a fifty-three-foot trailer from one location to another, drop it off for unloading or loading, and hook up another trailer and take it where it needs to go. We do that, as well, and that's what some shippers want—transport services as a low-cost commodity. But Nick Hobbs, who has been with JBHT since 1984 and now is president of DCS, points out that our experience helped us develop the expertise that sets us up to expand into other markets.

"The business we try to develop is the more challenging private fleets," Nick points out. "We say the more difficult the better, because we can operate it well, we can recruit the drivers, pay them well, and there's not as much competition in that area."

CHAPTER 6

The End Is Near . . . Always

The end is near and it's going to be awesome!
— Kevin D. Williamson, author

S helley Simpson admits she was a bit perplexed in 2007 when we asked her to take on the challenge of starting Integrated Capacity Solutions (ICS). Every other aspect of our company was asset-based, but this would be an animal of an entirely different breed. She wasn't very familiar with this animal, but what she knew about it she didn't exactly hold in high esteem.

"I had been trained that brokers were cheap and that they were brand-damaging," she recalled. "It could have been a shallow perspective, but that's what I thought about brokers."

Shelley's promising career at JBHT began in 1994 as a customer service representative, and she moved up quickly by working hard and demonstrating a great talent for understanding pricing and economics. Virtually all her experience revolved around asset-based businesses, because that was the core of the JBHT model. We served customers' freight logistics needs almost exclusively with the equipment we owned, not by brokering business to multiple external vendors. And as senior vice president of finance and administration, Shelley already had a really nice gig when we asked her to venture into the land of the great unknown called ICS.

"I was coming out of a billion-dollar segment that was very successful to start, almost from scratch, a part of the organization that we had been trained to think wasn't that great of a business," she said. "But Kirk said, 'We think it's a billion-dollar business, and we think you can get it there, so go get 'em tiger.' I believed in Kirk. I believed in our leadership. I believed in our company. Plus, I had been involved in pricing and working with customers for so long that I knew what our customers were asking for because I was there when they were asking for it."

The customers were asking for it. That was the key. There are times in business when you need to avoid the flavor of the month ideas and stick to what you do best. In the 1990s, we had to get rid of several distractions and focus on a few core businesses. But companies can become myopic at times, and when that happens, the competition—usually a start-up that took flight from someone's garage—quickly passes them.

Creative destruction is inevitable in business. Economist Joseph Schumpeter coined that term in 1942 to describe what he viewed as an "essential facto about capitalism"—that innovation inevitably replaces outdated product and process. The question is, who will innovate? Competition over time drives the creation of alternatives to existing products and services. That's why buggy manufacturers went out of business. And that's why J.B. Hunt Transport supplanted so many of the trucking industry's legacy carriers in the wake of deregulation.

Most businesses, and industries for that matter, take a reactive approach to creative destruction, and it inevitably costs them. Why? Because they are afraid to cannibalize their current business offerings for the sake of their future success. When companies don't operate with that fear, however, they are freed to develop purple segments through creative destruction from within.

When we partnered with the railroads for Intermodal, for instance, it took away from our core truckload business. But no segment illustrates our willingness to creatively destruct more than ICS. By setting up a segment that essentially works as a broker in the freight industry, we inevitably took business away from Truck, Intermodal, and DCS. Given the conditions of the market, however, we could see that it was "us or someone else." Our customers were asking for a solution we couldn't deliver, so the choice was simple: Adjust and deliver what they wanted or watch that business go to another company. And our background and experiences in Truck, DCS, and Intermodal positioned us perfectly to get in front of the "someone else's" of the world.

Shelley knew all of this, which is why she never balked at the new role with ICS. She helped create our innovative pricing model for the truckload segment, and during that process we all realized that our focus on the asset-based business was costing us opportunities with customers. We built huge efficiencies around driving the best routes and providing great service, but our customers now wanted more help with logistics and with lanes that weren't part of our business model. A customer would ask us to bid on a project for a hundred lanes, for instance, and we'd end up price competitive on no more than fifteen to twenty. Why? Because we didn't serve a particular area or we didn't have specific types of equipment. By necessity, we started working with other carriers, subcontracting them to handle pieces of the business that were outside of our lanes. That led us to launch ICS.

Resisting Destruction

The typical pushback against creative destruction within a company is that it cannibalizes your existing businesses. But we've never been concerned about cannibalizing one part of the company to offer a better solution for the customer. If there's a better solution for the customer, we need to offer it. Most companies won't do that. If we had seen ourselves as a "trucking company," we might have limited our options. Instead, we saw ourselves as a company that helped customers move freight, and we weren't—and aren't—limited in how we go about it.

When we started Intermodal, for instance, we knew it potentially would reduce the business for our Truck segment. But we took an all-in approach and looked at how the business would impact the company overall. We believed that doing what made the most sense for the customer would ultimately benefit us. Did Intermodal cannibalize Truck? It didn't matter. We were willing to trim our trucking fleet to give the customers what they needed, knowing it would offer the biggest return for us and our shareholders.

Plus, we knew the market. Customers wanted Intermodal for long-haul freight for two primary reasons. One, it typically was less expensive because, among other things, fuel was not as big of a piece of the cost as it was for over-the-road. And, two, trains had a smaller carbon footprint, so intermodal was much greener. We eventually developed a calculator that showed how much less carbon emissions happened when you converted a load of freight from over-the-road to Intermodal. That attracted customers in an increasingly environmentally conscious market.

With driver shortages, rising fuel costs, and the desire among shippers for a better option for moving freight long distances, the Truck business faced some steep challenges. Sure, embracing Intermodal meant less long-haul business for our Truck segment, but if we hadn't provided that option, no doubt someone else would have.

Shelley quickly caught the vision for taking a similar approach with ICS. She loves to build things, she's creative, futuristic, and loves a challenge. The idea of taking on CH Robinson, the big player in the freight brokerage space, fueled her fire. (She says I stoked that fire a bit by saying things like, "You're as good as CH Robinson, aren't you, Shell?" And, well, I suspect she's right.) Shelley recognized that our asset-based foundation provided unique advantages that would quickly catapult us toward success.

As the president of ICS, Shelley spent her first two months building a leadership team and doing market research to create a business plan. There was no book to guide her, but she thrived on the idea that she got to write the book. And she created a value proposition that was unique because it didn't come from a book, it came by starting with a blank page and simply figuring out what made the most sense. She realized ICS had to become "modal indifferent"—in other words, agnostic to how we would move a shipment.

"We were not in business to support our trucking company," she said. "We were in business to support our customers by serving the customer with the best answer possible in the market."

Others within the company weren't so enthusiastic about this new segment. Creative destruction isn't easy, because people worry about how it will impact their job security. It's only natural that emotions play a role.

"Those were some hard times," Shelley told us. "People were stressed because of the conflict that was occurring between being a large trucking company and being in the non-asset space. They thought we were competing against ourselves. That was hard for me, because I am extremely loyal and I would never want to do anything that would damage our brand. So those were very difficult conversations."

One senior-level meeting left Shelley visibly frustrated by the resistance she was getting from another part of the organization. She "popped off" during the meeting (her words) and fumed her way back to her office when it ended. She had barely settled into her chair when in walked her boss, Craig Harper.

"I don't get it," she told him. "We've gone over this and over this and over this. How can they not get it? It's exhausting."

Craig listened patiently and then said, "You know, I've never been on a ride in your car. Let's go to Starbucks."

Shelley took a deep breath.

"I get it," she said. "Am I getting the ice cream talk?"

The ice cream talk is when a leader takes someone out for ice cream (or coffee, as the case might be) to let them vent and remind them that everything will be okay. How can you feel too bad about the world when you're enjoying a double-scoop or sipping on a caramel mocha latte?

"Don't worry about everybody who thinks you can't be successful," Craig told Shelley. "Keep doing what you're doing and eventually ICS will be fully integrated into the culture of the company."

Shelley reflects on that conversation with great appreciation, because it illustrates a great point about how leaders implement creative destruction.

"You need your advocates when you're trying to change an organization," she said. "People don't always know they're pushing on you. And everything isn't perfect when you're starting from scratch. Add it all up and, well, you have to keep a positive attitude and you have to have advocates."

We got everyone on the same page by clearly communicating what we were doing and why, repeatedly, with an emphasis on the long-term view. It was a lot of work. We reminded them of the success of Intermodal, emphasized the importance each segment played in the success of the others, and painted a dynamic vision for the company's future if ICS were successful. Everyone needed to see their place in that future, or, as John Roberts pointed out, they'll never fully buy in.

"Don't let people get scared," John said. "That's how we get resistance. If I give customers self-service, do my account reps get scared and think they'll lose their jobs? That can't be part of our culture. We've hired people every year. We don't fire people here."

Despite the initial resistance, Shelley was the perfect person to lead the ICS segment. She had worked in the Truck segment. She had a background in customer service. She had worked with Intermodal and pricing. She brought credibility to the table, and everyone in the room knew she had the best interests of the company at heart.

"You weren't talking to someone from Mars," she told us. "I knew what was good for JBHT and what wasn't. We could articulate that these were two different types of businesses that would complement each other. We focused on what would be good for both parts. If we had enough business in ICS, that would help our trucking company with business on the day to day. Instead of begging someone else for freight, we would have freight. If you keep that competition in house, you will always have the best answer for your customers."

This approach led to success. Within two years, ICS was moving more than three hundred loads a day, which Shelley describes as "a big deal organizationally" because "it told people we weren't a niche business. People doubted us, whether they said it or not. So that milestone was a bit of validation."

The other key mark, she said, came in 2012 when ICS became a top five third-party logistic provider, according to *Inbound Logistics*. "That changed the mind-set of how customers viewed us," she said. JBHT has been in the top ten every year since 2010 and as high as tied for fourth in 2014. And in the first quarter of 2018, ICS was moving 3,961 shipments per day.

Patience amid Destruction

Most companies can't pull off this type of creative destruction. Even if they are willing to take the risk, they aren't patient enough to stick with it. When you blow things up, there's usually a bit of a mess. It takes time to clean it up and turn the chaos into productive, profitable order. Some companies simply aren't willing to mess with the mess, so they play it safe.

"Protectionism is the greatest risk we have," John pointed out. "If we get too attached or too enamored of our businesses, then they will kill us, because somebody out there is going to disrupt."

That attitude has to become a living part of the organization's culture. Too often, leaders call for innovation or disruption but dive for cover when things don't go well. They shift blame, pull the plug on projects, fire people, and give up. When that happens, the culture is sailing on a rudderless ship. There's disruption, but it's the culture that's exploding—along with any chances of innovative success.

"Your leadership at the very top has to be committed to a long-term view," Shelley said. "If we miss on the numbers this month because we're doing something for the long-term plan, you can't get beat up for it."

I remember broadcasting to the stock market that ICS would be $1 billion in revenue by 2012. We didn't make it until 2017, but we were well on our way, and, thanks to Shelley's leadership, it was being built in the right way. Goals often need adjusting. You rarely, if ever, hit them on the nose. In the case of ICS, missing the exact date we would hit $1 billion was less important than achieving steady growth fueled by satisfied customers at an appropriate margin.

"When we do the right thing for the customer all the time, we reinvent ourselves on a regular basis," Shelley said. "Who can come in and surprise us? We should never be surprised. But you have to have the right tone at the top."

That tone creates a culture that values grace, an essential ingredient for innovation. Operationally, JBHT has developed a ton of standardized processes that create efficiencies and allow us to scale. At the same time, we look for ways to drive out waste and improve, and that doesn't happen unless people are willing to take ownership of their work and take risks that disrupt the status quo. When you invite risks, you invite mistakes. How leaders react to those mistakes determines whether people will continue to take the risks.

"There's an amazing amount of grace to make mistakes," said Mark Greenway, our head of HR. "Nobody plays a perfect game. You're going to make a mistake. Just own it, have integrity, and don't make the same mistake over and over. So, we have developed this culture that adapts well to change. If you don't like change, don't come to J.B. Hunt. You know it's okay to make a mistake. And when you miss a tackle, you're going to get corrected and go back into the game."

CHAPTER 7

Living the Life Cycle

Control your own destiny or someone else will.
—Jack Welch, former CEO of GE

S hortly after John Roberts became CEO in 2011, he presented a rather interesting gift to each of the members of his executive team—a Crayola Color Wonder Magic Light Brush Kit.

Here's how it worked: You dipped the brush in one of the six paint options, but the color only emerged when you brushed it onto special paper. Parents would love it, right? Their kids could paint the house red—or any of the five other colors—but it wouldn't leave a mark unless they used the special paper. Mess-free coloring!

But why was a forty-six-year-old, newly appointed CEO handing out fancy, schmancy versions of crayons to his fellow executives?

"I was fascinated by the newness of such an old idea," he said when we asked him to retell the story.

John presented the gifts during one of his first meetings with his executive team. Then he took his Magic Light Brush and wrote a message that came to life on the paper. It said, "A new way to put color on the page."

By now, JBHT was more than thirty years old as a company, so John wanted to make an important point about the maturing organization. "Nothing has an eternal life cycle except for our souls," John said. "Everything has a maturation curve." JBHT had a history of innovation and both an "obligation and duty" to be entrepreneurial, so it was important that he established a tone from the beginning that the company's vision had to match the times and the competition.

"Nothing lasts forever," he said. "Even the greatest of ideas will age and deteriorate. There's always got to be a new way to put color on a page."

When John looks at the business segments that make JBHT stand out, he's constantly evaluating where they are in the lifecycle curve—introduction, growth, maturation, or decline. This curve, or some version of it, is most often used as a descriptor for a product life cycle, but as John points out, it applies more broadly. In Stage 0, a business generates an idea—a product, service, or business process. In Stage 1, the idea is introduced—tested, refined, and launched. In Stage 2, growth and demand accelerate as the market expands. There's growth accompanied by revenues and profits. Stage 3 brings maturity, as demand levels off. Finally, in Stage 4 the business declines. Customers have moved on, sales begin to thin, and what once was the cool, new big idea becomes a relic destined for a museum.

The only variable in the life cycle is time. That's the "x" axis. Whether it's a product, a service, or an entire business, it starts as an idea and eventually is introduced, grows, matures, and declines. But when and at what rate for each phase? Those are the questions that keep leaders up at night. Each phase requires different strategies, investment levels, and approaches from leadership. Recognizing where different business segments are in the curve, not being deceived by current, random changes, and leading the businesses appropriately have been key to JBHT's past and no doubt will be to its future.

Sometimes companies think a product or service is in decline when it is actually still in the maturity phase, causing them to sell the segment too early. Sometimes companies think it is in decline when it is still in the growth stage. Misreading where a product or service is in the product life cycle is a common mistake. It is easy to be deceived by current random changes in demand or changes in aggregate demand that affect local demand.

For instance, the Intermodal business had a slow introduction phase followed by a relatively fast growth phase.

"Right now, that curve is very smooth," John pointed out. "I'm starting to appreciate that the curve may have some plateaus and re-accelerations."

In other words, these stages are not always so neatly ordered. Periodically a new growth phase may occur after a maturity phase. Intermodal is a radically unique business. The barriers to entry are extremely high and the value proposition is so great in terms of economics and scale that it's likely to maintain sustained periods of growth before reaching maturation.

What difference does it make for a leader?

Well, if we believe Intermodal is moving into the maturation phase, we would likely invest differently. We might treat it more as a cash-cow model where we invest less in technology and equipment, but instead harvest the dollars that come from previous investments. After all, if you invest heavily in a mature business, you won't see significant returns on that invested capital. If investment is cut off too soon, however, the door is opened for competitors to take market share from a business that still has growth potential.

"We've learned that being a market leader is very valuable and should be protected—even as near-term profit declines, which is very unpopular with certain constituencies like shareholders," John told us. "I keep a very clear line of sight to the market share we have in equipment. My belief is that we should have that same or better market share in volume and revenue. If we keep that in balance, we won't harm pricing. That will allow us to maintain the right balance and not have to use our pricing power to keep our market share."

Know Where You Are on the Curve

The downfall of many successful companies comes partly because they don't adjust appropriately based on their position in this lifecycle curve. It's not just that a once-fabulous product grows stale and falls out of fashion. The bigger issue is that the company never saw it coming and the culture never reinvented itself so it could survive in a changed environment.

What you'll notice throughout the JBHT story is a culture that's always looking for the next big thing. That was the mindset of our founder, but founders retire and move on, and new leaders often overcompensate. In an effort to calm the storms the visionary founder created, the new leaders pull their ship into quiet and safe harbor where they can focus on execution. But then they leave it there until dry rot sets in. JBHT has always been able to reintroduce that innovative quality that creates a few storms. At times, the market demanded it. But many organizations are blind to such demands, especially when they involve leaving a comfortable space. Our people—at all levels of the organization—have always understood that slipping into the status quo isn't healthy, fun, or rewarding.

There's some risk in creating a culture that values moving quickly, because you can, and mostly likely will, get it wrong from time to time. But it's part of our DNA at J.B. Hunt Transport. As John put it, "We need to be on to the next thing. We feed on that." Intermodal, Dedicated Contract Services, and Integrated Capacity Solutions are all examples of how the JBHT culture said, "Feed me. Give me something new. Show me a new way of doing business."

Ideas like Final Mile (our home delivery service) and J.B. Hunt 360 (our web-based portal for shippers and drivers) are emerging as new ways to feed that culture.

But the risk is that a service you think is in decline is really still in growth or maturity. Causal variables can make it look like you are in decline or make a service that is in the introductory stage appear as though it is failing. Careful evaluation of these causal variables—changes in GDP, the interest rate, the price of oil, or regulatory changes—will help to properly identify your position in the product life cycle. It's also important to keep an optimistic and innovative spirit, because where you are on the product life cycle should not be taken as a given. With realistic optimism and an innovative spirit, you can change the shape of the curve.

One of John's primary roles as CEO is keeping that spirit alive. When we interviewed him for this book, he and his team had recently returned from an off-site retreat where they spent time studying two different books on innovating when you're a mature company.

"We need the challenge of innovation to keep the company's momentum," he said. "This is corny to say, but when you think you've got it figured out, it's time to hang it up. You gotta know you don't know. We can't be in love with anything we're doing right now. Today's world is demanding that we cannibalize the old ways of doing business. That doesn't mean we throw it out. You can reinvent it. But you can't be in love with it. If you're in love with it, it's going to eat you alive."

John understands the balance between an innovative spirit and the reality of a mature market.

As John points out, the discipline that leaders must apply to return on invested capital can easily stifle innovation. You must figure out how to break down those paradigms without breaking down the company and losing the power system of cash flow generated off your current businesses.

Many companies fail at this. John's favorite example is Blockbuster, which for the benefit of you younger readers, once owned the market for movie rentals with its brick-and-mortar stores. Then Netflix came along, first with subscription-based, mail-delivered videos and then with a video-streaming approach. After building some momentum, the leaders at Netflix called the folks at Blockbuster around 2000 with hopes of selling their innovative little jewel to the market leader for $50 million. Netflix would then manage Blockbuster's online brand, and Blockbuster would promote Netflix in the stores.

That's OK, the folks from Blockbuster said. *We've got a great gig going. People like coming into the stores for popcorn and a movie. This mail order stuff won't last and streaming won't work.*

Blockbuster didn't recognize that it was in the maturity phase and headed toward decline. They were blind to the impact and opportunities of new technologies and customer preferences. Netflix, on the other hand, had incubated and was ready to grow. Ten years later, Blockbuster went bankrupt and Netflix had grown into a $28 billion business and a market leader.

Here's the question John posed to his leadership team, and a question other leaders would do well to ask: "What part of our conversations sound like that? What part sounds like I'm the guy who automatically says, 'I'll pass?'"

There are times when you should pass, of course, but innovators explore new options more deeply and look for every possible way to turn what might seem a bit crazy into a workable business advantage.

"Think about something like opening our web system to other carriers so we can make them better," John said. "You might say, 'Now, wait a minute. I can't allow someone else to get better on my investment.' Okay, but what if we captured that capacity and created loyalty with that carrier and then resold that capacity to our customers and made a profit on it? That's not so scary anymore because that's a viable way to do business. 'But that means maybe one of our trucks might sit.' Okay, so maybe we don't buy more trucks."

How you perceive a business segment can affect how you change the curve of the product life cycle. If Blockbuster had seen itself in the entertainment business rather than the videotape and DVD rental business, then it could have shifted its service to be more like Netflix and thus changed the shape of its life cycle.

The point is, an innovative culture doesn't allow itself to say, "That's scary" or "We've got it all figured out" or "We've always done it this way." Instead, it's willing to make dramatic changes to a business segment. When a business segment moves into maturity, it begins to groan. If you'll listen, here's what it's really saying: "I don't want to do it this way. It hurts. Fix me. Change my product life cycle curve."

CHAPTER 8

Total Engine Maintenance

That engine rattles like a goat in a can pile.
— Bob Ralston, JBHT EVP-Maintenance (retired)
and resident philosopher

The early 2000s proved to be watershed years for JBHT's truckload business, and the impact reverberated throughout every segment of the company in ways that weren't always that obvious.

As you might have gathered by now, the truckload business is tough. There are hundreds of competitors who are after the same business *and* the same qualified drivers. And with rare exception, the truckload industry has a shortage of qualified drivers. In addition to costs of recruiting, hiring, training, paying, and supporting drivers, the price of fuel is a significant expense. Then there's the capital investment—trucks, trailers, containers, and other equipment, none of which come cheap. Many truckload operators happily exist on a cash-flow model. They charge the lowest possible price to get the business, then survive the best they can so long as the cash flow keeps their nose above water.

The more we looked at our returns for the truckload business in the late 1990s, the more we saw it as unhealthy for the company. We found ourselves competing on price to win business, then turning a razor-thin profit that made all the effort hardly seem worth it. Bob Ralston, our executive vice president in charge of maintenance back then, summed it up in his own unique style with a story from earlier in his life when he and his brother operated an auto repair shop.

"We were always busy," Bob would say, "but we were never making any money. Finally, I told my brother, 'Gosh, if we're going to starve to death, I'd at least like to be rested.'"

That's the way the truckload business often felt. We weren't exactly starving to death, because the other segments of our business were doing well. But we were working harder than ever in the truckload business for scant returns. Something had to give. If you're going to invest hard-earned money—shareholders' money, money the company has made from other things—you have to make sure you're getting an adequate return. And when we evaluated the business, we realized we weren't getting an adequate return. All we were doing was following the low-price crowd and killing ourselves to stay competitive. We were doing the same thing over and over and expecting different results, which is the definition of stupidity. Or insanity. Or both.

Finally, we said enough was enough.

That's when we bucked the industry by applying two important but extremely difficult and counterintuitive business principles: One, the customer is most certainly not always right. They are always to be respected, listened to, and served, but only when a return is generated. And, two, the best sales tool in the world is indifference. *You want to buy this watch? Here's the price. You don't like that price? Okay, see you later.* That's the conclusion we came to on the truck side. Let's be indifferent. Let's make sure the price we quote is going to have a fair return to it, even if it costs us business.

The truckload business is somewhat of a commodity, but customers really want three things: They want capacity—the ability to pick up and deliver their load when and where they need it. They want good service. And they want a competitive price. Most shippers do competitive bids to determine who will get their business, and most of the truckload companies, then and now, lead with price. But the people who give the lowest price, then and now, often can't provide the other two things. They don't have the capacity at peak times or they don't have the service to get the job done adequately. Those were our biggest advantages at JBHT. We had all this capacity where these shippers needed it, and we provided great service. So, why did we go to the lowest common denominator on price?

Because we were like the lion in *The Wizard of Oz*—we lacked c-c-c-c-courage!

So, we summoned up some c-c-c-c-courage and started pricing in a way that provided a decent return. Shelley Simpson, Terry Matthews, and I led the effort. Craig Harper remembers seeing us gathered in a conference room for entire days in meetings with the pricing and sales teams going over proposals in detail to make sure we had the pricing right.

"Kirk had this long ruler and you'd see him in there with a big printout going line by line through all the bids and all the rates and making changes," Craig said. "We got real serious about the rates we were charging. We had *a lot* of meetings about the rates we were charging."

Frankly, it was a great time. I enjoyed it, because it started producing results. As with any significant change, of course, those results didn't come immediately. Freight bids typically are yearly or multiyear, so it takes time to implement new pricing and more time to see the results. You have to go through a year's worth of repricing, maybe longer, all the while holding your ground. And holding your ground isn't easy. When you raise your rates, you inevitably make people unhappy—and not just the customers who you ask to pay a higher rate. I vividly recall one pricing review meeting during which the salesman was literally sweating as we raised our bid for the work he was in charge of selling. Salesmen want to win the business. All of it. That's their job—to go out and sell. From his perspective, we were pricing ourselves out of the business.

"How much of this business do you want to win?" he finally asked in frustration.

"However much provides us a reasonable return on our investment," we told him. "If that's zero, then so be it."

Many of our customers claimed price was not the main component when they evaluated bids, but their behaviors betrayed those words. When I asked one customer rep how he rated the factors like service and capacity, he said, "Well, it's complicated." I told him I was a CPA so maybe it wouldn't be too complicated for me. He and I both knew that price was driving his decision. So, we lost some business, at least on the front end. But something amazing happened. We got most of it back and we became much more profitable.

The most powerful example involves a major customer that shipped tons of products to various retailers all over the country. We had done about $28 million in business with this customer the previous year, and we had made some money . . . but not nearly enough. So, when we rebid for the work, we priced it with our new model to ensure we would earn a solid return. Not long after the bids went out, we got a call from the company's head of traffic. She wanted to come for a visit, so she and her entourage flew down to Arkansas and gathered with us in a conference room for some hand-wringing.

"We just want you to know how poorly you did with this bid," she told us.

"Well, how much did we win?" I asked.

"You only won $2 million of the business," she said.

"Oh, I'm surprised," I said, I guess rather arrogantly. "I didn't think we'd win that much."

We didn't change our mind. We didn't ask to reprice it. Instead, we told them we were fine with the $2 million we'd earned. We thanked them for the business, and we bid them adieu. But that year I think we did $24 million in business with that company because they had to come to us when the lower-priced carriers ran out of capacity. And when they did, we used our higher "back-up" pricing. We ended up doing about the same amount of business but at a much higher level of profitability.

As we increased our profitability, we also were able to "trade up" when it came to the freight we hauled for our customers. We had learned to evaluate and prioritize our customers because not only is the customer not always right, but not all customers are the same. We couldn't turn bad business into good business, but we could trade up bad business for better business and then trade up that better business for even better business.

Plenty of people in the industry thought we were crazy with this pricing model. They were sure we were going to run ourselves out of the truckload business. "Nobody's going to pay that price," they said. But they did pay the price. Maybe not at first and maybe not willingly. I remember one guy at a retailer we worked with getting so irritated he called us "effing pirates." But we weren't taking advantage of them. We were just doing the right thing.

Pricing, to me, is a fundamental underpinning of business in general, but certainly the transportation business. It had grown critically out of whack in the truckload business. I'm convinced that people in business frequently make the mistake of not charging enough. They price to the market, which is the lowest common denominator. If you've got a good product and good service and can deliver on your promises, you need to charge a reasonable price.

Of course, that takes courage. You can't be scared that you're going to lose the business if it's a bad price. And, frankly, if the only thing we were doing was truckload, I'm not sure we would have had the courage to raise our rates. We should have had the courage to do it, but it would have been harder. What made it easier was the fact that we were looking at one segment of our business. It wasn't our only source of business. Also, we were intentionally shrinking our truckload business at that time, primarily because the return on invested capital (ROIC) was inadequate. But, again, that comes down to proper analysis and getting your head straight. We weren't going to work for free. It takes some belief and courage to make that decision.

Ultimately, our pricing structure changed the industry. Not totally, but we got some apostles from it, particularly when they saw it showing up in the financial results. And regardless of what the industry thought or how our competitors reacted, it was absolutely the right decision and a turning point for truckload business. It shored up that segment of our business, and it spilled over into our other segments because it shaped our companywide view toward earning an adequate return.

Our philosophy around pricing doesn't just apply to truckload. It was exaggerated in truckload because they were doing so poorly during that time. But we try to price all of our business the way it should be done. Sometimes that results in losing business to less sophisticated, indifferent competitors who are willing to do it for less than us. But our profitability hinges on having the courage to give up the things that don't serve our best interests anyway.

Working the Systems

Very few business leaders understand, much less apply, systems theory. For JBHT, it seemed to come naturally, perhaps because the nature of our business requires a focus on things like total engine maintenance. Businesses, like engines, are complex, so you have to understand how all of the pieces work together. You can't just change the oil regularly and call it good. You have to service the entire truck.

Systems theory took off in academic settings shortly after World War II as researchers across a variety of disciplines in the 1940s and 1950s began to study systems with interrelated and interdependent parts. They wanted to understand how change in one part of a system affected other parts and the whole, with the goal of managing those systems more effectively.

J.B. Hunt Transport is a complex system of business segments that serve customers with complex systems and needs. One of our strengths through the years has been the ability to take a holistic view of our systems—like how pricing in truckload impacts the company's overall profitability—and a holistic view of our customers' systems.

It's common, for instance, to find leaders throughout an organization who are searching for ways to minimize their costs. It's rare, however, to find leaders who look for ways to minimize the total, systemwide cost, taking into account the interactions between the costs. For example, a lot of companies have transportation managers whose key metric is how much they spend on transportation. Thus, they typically want to ship in large quantities because that saves money on shipping. But shipping in large quantities increases inventory costs, which works against the goals of the managers who are responsible for inventory because their key metric is minimizing inventory cost. A systems approach accounts for both metrics—and other metrics, as well—before deciding the best possible strategy.

Internally, we've taken a systems approach to each segment of our business and to the company as a whole. In the 1970s and 1980s, we became one of the best truckload operators in the nation because we focused on the three critical elements: utilization of productivity, measured by miles per truck per day; keeping our empty miles as low as possible; and keeping costs as low as possible. Excelling in one of those areas wasn't enough. Excelling in all three created phenomenal earnings for a small company and put us on the radar of investment banks that wanted to take the company public.

As time went on and the truckload environment became less profitable, we realized the need to dramatically change our approach to pricing—and, as already noted, that had an impact not only on the industry but on the other segments of our business. DCS, for instance, adopted a philosophy of "bill what you pay and pay what you bill." That segment is pretty much a cost-plus business. First, you have to know what your costs are. That takes analytical ability and it takes people doing the pricing who understand how to make money in a business and who don't just follow their competitors. You have to know what your costs are and pass those cost on, plus a return. Pricing under your cost is suicide. It might be a slow death, but it results in eventual suicide. And customers will let you do it. Why wouldn't they?

In DCS, this pricing approach led us away from the easier, more commodity-like, low-price customers and toward what we consider the much more difficult jobs that require more of the expertise and proprietary systems technology that our competitors lack. We traded generic, easier, and less profitable work for more challenging but more profitable work, and the bottom line reaps the benefits. If it's easy anyone can do it, and you end up looking just like every other company in the industry.

Throughout JBHT, we differentiate ourselves from the competition by our quality of service, our proprietary technology, our experience, and our ability to add value through a systems approach that uses the strengths of the entire company. We compete on price at times, but it's not the backbone of our model.

"One of the things we tell customers is we won't be the cheapest, but we're going to create the most value," Shelley said. "Customers know when we quote a price that we will stand on our word. We will deliver on our promise. That's different than the industry. We used to call it 'allocations.' If you made a commitment to us and said you were going to give us five loads a day, we would load in that commitment. When we would start booking shipments for customers, even if the market heated up and a customer was willing to pay us three times the amount of the other customer, we fulfilled those commitments first. Our customers knew that. We're known to have a premium on our brand. Now we have better answers. We're not the cheapest broker. We don't want to be the cheapest broker. We want to create the best value."

Beyond Pricing

The systems approach isn't just about pricing. It's also apparent in our culture. We don't see JBHT as a bunch of individual business segments that spin their own little cocoons and insulate from one another. Functionally, we're one family that rises and falls together.

That's why the bonus plan hinges on overall performance and it's why we use long-term incentives like restricted stock to motivate the team to think like owners of the company. And it's why cross-team communication is so vital to our success. Each of our segments learns from the mistakes and successes of the other. And, perhaps more important, each of our segments helps support and sell the other. This is an approach we call *modal indifference*, which, as noted earlier, I credit to Shelley from her time launching ICS. The idea is that no matter which segment you sell for JBHT, you're expected to offer the segment or segments that work best for the customer.

If a big customer has a lot of freight, it might make sense to move it by truck, but it might make more sense to move some or all of it by intermodal. If you're a typical trucker, you never offer that option because you want to haul everything by truck. But intermodal has enormous advantages in certain situations. Or maybe a dedicated option is needed. Or maybe you need to provide trucks you don't own through ICS. At some point along the way, we start talking about providing solutions. We found that often the customers don't know what solutions they need or even that they need a solution. They are locked into a customary way of operating and don't realize a better way exists. It's our job to show them.

This reminds me of Jun-Sheng Li, a former senior vice president for Walmart's e-commerce who once ran logistics for us. Jun has an incredible personal story that saw his family in China forced into exile because his father published a newspaper that ran opinions counter to the government's liking. His father went to jail, while Jun, his mother, and his sister were sent to the Gobi Desert, where they literally had wolves at their door. He learned English by listening to a transistor radio at night, and he eventually worked his way to America and into a job with J.B. Hunt Transport.

Perhaps because of that background, Jun had a way of saying whatever he was thinking without upsetting people. One day we were meeting with a big-box retailer that specializes in home improvement products when Jun basically told them they didn't know what they were doing. Then he gave them a solution for how they could do things better.

Jun had great ideas about ways to optimize freight. In fact, his "big ball theory"—that if we had access to data on all the freight in the country we could optimize it and put it with the right asset and reduce empty miles and backfills for perfect coordination—led to the creation of Transplace, the data-driven logistic provider JBHT co-founded in partnership with some other carriers. While we no longer own a stake in Transplace, we still use a data-driven, systems approach to managing every aspect of our business so that the customer gets the best possible solutions.

The systems approach to identifying solutions for our customers requires our sales teams to really understand our total business and the business of the customer they're approaching.

"I love to go see a customer who doesn't do business with us, because we're going to start with everything," said Shelley, who now is JBHT's president of highway services and chief commercial officer. "Starting in one mode makes me a direct competitor with the other person that only does one mode. We don't want to just compete against HUB Group, or CH Robinson, or Ryder, or Swift. We want to do all of it and have them compete against us."

When Shelley was leading ICS, she realized we needed a more strategic perspective of supply chain when it came to sales. She was along for one customer visit when the vice president charged with leading the conversation fell ill, leaving the lead sales person to step up. It was one of our top salesmen, but he had a very narrow view of what to offer because it was limited to the part of the business he typically sold.

"I recognized the gap at that moment," she said. "The light bulb came on. I thought, 'We only have eight people who can go do this work, versus putting together an entire sales organization that can do the work.' He was one of our very best sales people. Top of the pack. Everybody wanted to hire him. But I recognized a gap that was occurring inside him of connecting the way our customers think about the supply chain."

That's what led to retraining the entire sales team to think with modal indifference.

"The sales group went through a major transformation in being modal indifferent," she said. "The scenario is this: If speed is critical because they don't have enough lead time, even in a long length of haul, then intermodal might not be the viable solution. I have to understand the root of the issue. Once our team understood that, it really changed the way we went to market in a big way. We said, 'Let me see your data,' not, 'Let's talk about price.' I love to compete when we can get the in-house data."

When we put the right data into our system, we feel confident we'll come up with a solution that's worth the price to our customers and that drives profitability for our company. It is a perfect example of being purple on the inside.

CHAPTER 9

Competent to the Core

Humility and competence are the keys to a successful life.
— Clifford Cohen, author

G ary Hamel and C. K. Prahalad once defined three criteria for developing "core competencies" in a corporation: That it provides potential access to a wide variety of markets; that it makes a significant contribution to the perceived customer benefits of the end product; and that it is difficult to imitate by competitors.[1]

When you look at the history of JBHT, you find that as an organization we've always been pretty good at identifying our core competencies—things like our collective knowledge and experiences, our diverse skill sets, and our unique technologies and proprietary systems. We've also been pretty good at collaborating across the organization to create business advantages from those competencies. The purple cow business segments, in other words, have emerged from our core competencies.

When you look at the history of Dedicated Contract Services, however, you quickly discover that core competencies don't always spring to life overnight, nor do they create growth without a struggle. DCS operates or augments private fleets for customers, and it's easy to see the core competencies that provide this business with a competitive advantage. We're good at transportation, and most shippers are not. They want to focus on their core business, be it oil, plastics, retail, food services, manufacturing, or the like. So, they hand their freight transportation responsibilities—along with the risks—over to us. We operate fleets all over the country, some that don't even have the JBHT

---

1. Gary Hamel and C. K. Prahalad, "The Core Competence of the Corporation," *Harvard Business Review*, May/June 1990, available at https://hbr.org/1990/05/the-core-competence-of-the-corporation, accessed June 12, 2017.

logos on the trucks, and our expertise creates efficiencies and savings for our customers.

We have access to a wide variety of markets, we make a significant contribution that benefits our customers, and our services are difficult for competitors to imitate—pretty much the textbook definition of how you develop core competencies.

When we started DCS in 1993, however, we had very few of those advantages.

Mike Seals, one of the first college graduates to go through our management program, was leading our logistics business at the time, and he made the case for entering the dedicated logistics business. We didn't have the internal expertise to do it on our own, so we looked for outside help. We hired two veterans in that segment of the industry, and they built a team of mostly external recruits who launched DCS for us.

Within four years, DCS had grown to a $175 million operation, but, as you might recall from an earlier chapter, the group in many ways was operating as an independent company. It had its own headquarters in Atlanta, for instance, and its leadership had a different bonus structure from the rest of our team. Our bonus and stock options have always been tied to the entire company's performance, not separated by unit. When it became clear that DCS would have to align with the rest of J.B. Hunt Transport, the leadership within DCS rebelled. One morning in July 1997 we walked into work and found nineteen faxes—the top nineteen people who were running DCS had resigned en masse and were going out on their own.

Of course, we weren't sure how we would survive, but we knew we could figure it out! And we did so by leaning into our existing core competencies and building new ones.

A Battlefield Promotion

As it turned out, John Roberts was the right guy at the right place at the right time.

Well, he wasn't actually at the right place at the right time. He was on vacation in Florida with his family when the resignations came rolling in like NASCAR drivers barreling toward the finish line at Daytona. But he was without question the right guy.

John had been with JBHT since 1989, mostly in a sales role. When we launched DCS, he joined that team as a salesman and helped start a couple of sizable fleets. He knew how to sell DCS, but he had learned about the operations, too. In fact, he points out that he learned a great deal about operations when he "broke a fleet" and spent months helping to fix it.

"I didn't have to, but I felt obligated to help fix it because I had sold it," John said. "That proved to be a great education for later, because I had some credibility with the operations people."

In 1995, John took a role working with Paul Bergant, who at that time was vice president of marketing strategy. John brought some of what he'd learned in DCS about pricing and service and helped Paul figure out how we could apply it to Intermodal and Truck pricing. (Another example of how core competencies filter throughout our organization.)

John heard about the mass resignations, so he knew changes were afoot. When he got a message from me while he was on vacation, he figured I was going to ask him to run the sales unit for DCS. I had something bigger in mind.

"The plane is on the way," I said when we finally connected. "We need you. You're gonna run the segment."

John didn't exactly leap at the opportunity. He was thirty-two years old and had never had more than five employees under his direct care. Plus, this would be a life-changing role that would be tough on his family, which then included children who were four and two.

"Kirk, I cannot take this job, yet," he told me. "I've got to talk to my wife, man. I gotta call you back."

John found his wife at "some terrible amusement park where she had taken the kids." They went to a nearby dive oyster bar to talk, and he didn't sugarcoat the opportunity.

"This is the deal," he told her. "This is going to be a train wreck! I'm going to be working long hours. You've got to be okay with this, or I'm not going to do it."

With her blessing, John called back and took the job. The plane was already on its way to take him to Atlanta as the new president of DCS. It was a classic battlefield promotion.

"Nobody was really sure I'd make it," John said, "but they thought, 'We've got nothing to lose, so let's give this kid a try.' So that's how we started running DCS."

What initially seemed like a pending disaster turned out to be a blessing in disguise and the best thing that could have happened to DCS, the company as a whole, and, of course, John.

Under John's direction, DCS took off.

"What happened in my mind was the right marriage of J.B. Hunt culture on top of a really, really good business model," John said. "Those guys had brought the model, but they didn't have the culture. I knew the culture. I grew up under Paul Bergant and Kirk Thompson and Jeff Franco and Mike Taylor and all of these guys who taught me the J.B. Hunt way. There's a great cultural power in the system here. You have to know it. And you can learn it. But they never bothered to learn it. It always got in their way."

That's the missing ingredient many organizations need when it comes to core competencies. It's not just about being good at something or having a unique product or services that others can't easily replicate. It's about having those things *plus* a culture that brings them to life—a culture that shares them, then makes the most of them with a selfless attitude that looks for ways to serve the customer, support employees, and grow the company as a whole.

With an infusion of JBHT culture into a solid business model and with favorable market conditions, DCS grew 30 to 40 percent a year for three or four years.

"It was kind of a rock show," John said. "We were killing the numbers. It's a fun business. We created a culture within a culture. It was fast and rock and roll, and it was good for J.B. Hunt."

The DCS rock show attracted top talent from throughout the JBHT ranks for several reasons. For starters, it's a very transparent business. You can easily see when you're winning and when you're not. The truckload business is hard because a lane often doesn't tell you everything you need to know, whereas a fleet can tell you everything you need to know. JBHT runs a unique P&L on every single DCS fleet—nearly seven hundred of them as of this writing—and the leaders know to the penny what each fleet makes every single month and every single quarter. In the early years, employees loved the fast pace and the idea of building something new that had so much momentum.

As with many rock stars, however, there came a day when the music died . . . or at least when the band got a bit off tune. As John put it, "We rocked-starred our way to a complete collapse and overplayed our hand in a number of ways." DCS built dozens of new fleets to address the tightening trucking market in the mid-2000s, including one with about five hundred tractors for a major retailer. It was a huge success . . . until the truckload market, as it always does, cycled. Pricing came down, capacity went up, and the demand for dedicated fleets hit a roadblock. The very good customer with the fleet of five hundred tractors exercised the termination clause in its contract and, poof—bye, bye Miss American pie. At the time, DCS operated around 2,500 trucks, so the idea of parking 20 percent of them wasn't easy to take.

"That would certainly be a strong candidate for my worst day," John said. "It taught us a lot of lessons, though, about not paying enough attention to what's building and how quickly it's building. If we go up real fast, we could come down real fast. This particular line of services went up too fast. Now, I would see that. In fact, I have. There's a large retailer out west that wanted us to go real fast about two years ago. We're managing that business with this in mind so we can slow that curve down. I know I'm pounding guys about growth, but you have to manage that curve or it will manage you. You have to say no, and it takes some experience to say no, especially when it's great business and you're making good money on it."

John learned a great deal from that experience and, in fact, the lessons he learned during that period helped him grow into the leader who would become JBHT's CEO. And, as he said, it also helped DCS refocus and find a more consistent, sustained path to growth. DCS became a distinctive business segment because we developed core competencies within JBHT and applied them in the right ways to the market so that what we did and how we did it became visibly unique in the eyes of our employees and customers.

From a technical perspective, we bring operational experience and research that few other companies can easily replicate. We use highly sophisticated analysis to help us efficiently run fleets, and our customers appreciate that expertise. This allows us to treat DCS as a non-commodity business, and that's what really separates us from our competition.

Most companies in the dedicated logistics business approach it as a very generic offering. The problem with generic services is it becomes a price game. It's like a commodity. Think oil or bauxite. The price is the price, and it's hard to gain an advantage when everybody provides the same thing. We migrated away from that intentionally, partly because losing the contract for that five-hundred-truck fleet taught us we had to do things others don't want to do. We needed to differentiate our services—apply the theory of differentiation—and then we tie them all together for the customer.

Some customers, of course, are in the market for the generic service. They want a white-label, low-cost brand—a service, for instance, that provides drivers who haul a fifty-three-foot trailer from a distribution center to a store, unhook it, and move on to the next job. We provide that service to those who want it. That's the easy part, which is why it's the approach most others take. The non-generic accounts, however, are much harder. A purple cow doesn't just look different, it *is different*. It does things other cows can't, partly because that's its nature—to embrace the more difficult business.

"We like stuff that other people have trouble doing," John said. "We've taught ourselves how to do it. We're very adaptable. You'll see our fleets look more complex than what you find our competition building. We have to do stuff that costs more money because we know how to make a return on investment."

DCS competes with private fleets by bringing capital, taking on liability and workers' compensation risks, and working with customers who need specialized equipment that often makes multiple stops and requires the drivers to do much more than drive from one location to another and unhook or hook up a trailer. For example, we run fleets that haul live chickens and chicken feed, which is far more difficult than typical drop-and-hook services. The feed trucks require trailers that cost about $200,000 each. The live haul trucks have cages. In addition to the capital density, these fleets present operational challenges, labor challenges, and systemic challenges. The drivers can work odd hours and often go off the beaten paths because that's where farms are located.

Another example involves the food services industry, where our trucks often deliver supplies late at night when no one is at the store. Our drivers have the keys to the building, unload the supplies, rotate the stock, mop their way to the door, and lock up on their way out. It's not easy to find, train, and supervise drivers for these fleets, or to manage the logistics efficiently.

"If there's a common thread," John pointed out, "it's that we have a culture that embraces difficulty and we've gotten good at it."

The Culture Competency

The culture aspect of our success in DCS can't be overstated, and John wasn't the only one who infused that culture. Not long after John took over DCS, he brought in Nick Hobbs as vice president of operations. Nick had worked in Truck and Intermodal, mainly dealing with drivers, and he had run our automotive fleet, which at the time ran about four hundred trucks that were dedicated to companies like Ford and General Motors. This background gave him the technical expertise to oversee operations in DCS. The holdovers from the original DCS team, however, were skeptical about another JBHT lifer stepping into such an influential position. Nick vividly recalls when he was introduced to the rest of the team during a monthly financial review meeting that John held on the patio of a country club not far from our headquarters.

"When we made that announcement, there were still a few people who were unhappy about all the changes," Nick recalled. "I can visualize their nervousness about what I was going to bring and what I was going to do."

They quickly learned to appreciate Nick's business acumen, but his JBHT heart and mind were even more important when it came to reshaping DCS. It's one thing to say you're going to tackle the harder jobs, but it's another to create a culture that wants to do it and, more important, can execute on it. That's the core competency Nick helped bring to DCS.

"My philosophy, which came from my time at automotive and came from Mr. Hunt, was that we were going to take great care of our customers," said Nick, who now is president of DCS. "We would listen and provide solutions for them. If we did that, if we took care of them, they would take care of us. That's the mind-set we try to instill. To do that, you have to take care of your people. So, we had that same mind-set with drivers and office employees. That's what we try to do, and that's the reason you see the tenure you see today—continuity, expertise, and great culture and values. That's what we started building from the beginning."

That approach to culture creates what John calls a "maniacal commitment to service." This might not seem like a core competency, since any company can commit to service. But let's face it: Most companies only commit to *the idea* of great service. Committing to the time, money, energy, and sacrifice that it takes to provide great service? Not so much.

"We're fanatical about it," John told us. "When you do business with us, you're going to get the right equipment every time. You're going to get trained people who are committed to safety and equipment that won't break down. We'll build the fleet as efficiently as it can be built, because we know how. That's hard to replicate, because you have to commit yourself to the experience."

One way JBHT does this is by investing in operations managers, the men and women who run a fleet from within the walls of a customer's facility, as well as managers who oversee geographic regions and help troubleshoot problems. The operations managers are all veteran employees with at least eight years of experience. They've grown up with their accounts. They know the dedicated business, but they also know the business of the customers they

serve. They become experts in the customer's industry, whether that's agricul-
ture, food, oil and gas, or something else. In many ways, they are as much a
part of the customer's organization as they are ours. They are on-site dealing
with rates, billing, invoices, hiring, training, safety, driver issues, customer
concerns, and, of course, leaders back at our corporate office. This approach
is expensive, because you have to recruit, train, and adequately pay managers
who typically oversee multi-million-dollar fleets and can do the work of a
CEO.

"They're basically running their own small business," Nick said.

These aren't easy jobs. You have to get the right people who can deal with
the drivers (who might be old enough to be their parents) but who also can
deal with the customers. Those are totally different personalities that require
different approaches. You have to be relatable to drivers, but you have to be
confident and precise with the customers when you're presenting an invoice
or in weekly staff meetings talking about transportation costs. We are extremely selective when recruiting these managers. We value people with great
work ethic, a sharp mind, and good people skills. That's hard to find. But we
pay well, offer a good bonus plan, and opportunities for advancement. So, we
get the best. And having the best people gives us advantages that are difficult
for others to duplicate.

Most of our competition prefers centralized locations for their fleet managers, but we see that as a brown cow approach. We believe our commitment in
this regard has a lot to do with our 98–99 percent retention rate with customers, which is by far the best in the industry. Once we get in, we tend to keep the
business because we're not just committed to the idea of great service—we're
committed to making it a reality.

Again, that track record didn't come overnight. We had to learn a few lessons the hard way. For instance, one day Nick got a phone call from a major
office supply chain that had decided to switch to another provider for one of
its facilities. Nick and John arranged a meeting with the executive who ran the
company's supply chain operations and quickly discovered why we had lost
that piece of business.

"His strategy was changing," Nick said, "and we were not connecting with it."

The company had gone from a focus on "service at all cost" to a focus on
balancing the service-to-cost ratio. Suddenly, we were providing very high-
end service to a customer who saw cost as a major factor. We were charging
a higher rate because we had extra trucks and drivers on standby to ensure

we hit a 99–100 percent success rate. With the strategy change, the customer would have been fine with a 97 percent rate if it reduced his costs.

Like all setbacks, this one provided an opportunity to improve and develop our core competency. After losing that business, we created a practice we call Customer Value Delivery, or CVD—a regularly scheduled process that ensures we stay in tune with our customers.

"That was a bad day that actually turned into a good thing for us in the long term," Nick said. "But it was painful at the time."

Competency's Offspring

The core competencies that helped turn DCS into a success are contributing to another segment within DCS that may soon be a purple cow on its own. Once again, it began with a willingness to listen to the needs of our customers. In 2006, our team was meeting with Brian Hancock, who at the time was vice president of supply chain for Whirlpool, to discuss the intermodal services we provided for them. As the meeting was wrapping up, we happened to ask them what other challenges they were facing.

"Well, we're having trouble with this final mile stuff," they told us.

We had no idea what "final mile stuff" was, so, of course, we asked.

"It's doing delivery and installation of appliances in people's homes," they told us.

That falls into the category of "the more difficult the better," so we asked them to let us see if we could provide some solutions. They agreed and gave us some data on the Little Rock, Arkansas, market. Then they held our hands as we ran two trucks.

"We cut our teeth on that for four-to-six months," Nick said. "We figured out how to hire for it and execute it."

We did well enough that they gave us Tulsa, Oklahoma; Springfield, Missouri; and Wichita, Kansas. When that went well, they handed us Los Angeles to see how we did with a larger market. And when that went well, they tossed us a "problem market"—a big city with all sorts of issues. It took nearly a year, but we stabilized that market, as well.

One evening Nick and John were leaving a meeting in Atlanta when John got a call on his cellphone from Brian at Whirlpool.

"I want you to meet us tomorrow at the Whirlpool hanger in Benton Harbor, Michigan," he said. "That's all I can tell you right now."

John, of course, was worried that there were service problems or, even worse, that we were losing the account.

"What's going on?" he asked Nick.

"I have no idea what's going on," Nick told him, "but I think we're good everywhere."

They went home and flew to Benton Harbor the next day. When they arrived, a small group of Whirlpool executives met them and told them they wanted JBHT to bid on their entire network. The meeting was held in the airplane hangar because they wanted to keep it secret. John, Nick, and Brad Hicks spent about six months leading the process of figuring out how to take over ninety LDCs (Local Distribution Centers) and coming up with pricing for the deal that ultimately was worth more than $175 million to our business.

"That was a great day," Nick said.

Indeed. And with the growth of e-commerce, large format home delivery—what we call final mile—is a $12 billion market that's continuing to expand. In addition to appliances, final mile deliveries also include things like furniture, bedding, fitness equipment, cabinets, and electronics. It's become a bigger and bigger piece of our DCS business. While there are more than 250 carriers who provide final mile service in the continental United States, 50 percent of those operate in three states or fewer. And less than 20 percent of them operate in at least thirty-six states. We're able to use our DCS experience, our network of distribution centers, an equipment base of more than 700 box trucks, and more than 1,500 employees to build a comingled network that covers the continental United States.

"The rule around here is it has to do a billion dollars," Nick said. "It's on the path to do that. In the next few years you'll see final mile spin out and become its own segment."

CHAPTER 10

Race Ahead of Technology

If you have everything under control, you're not moving fast enough.
— Mario Andretti, former race car driver

A nalyst John Larkin began following JBHT around the time we went public, so he has a deep appreciation for who we are as a company and how we got here, as well as a deep respect for our visionary founder.

John, who now is managing director for Stifel Transportation & Logistics Research Group, once visited Arkansas in the 1980s, and J.B. took him for a tour of the area. They climbed into J.B.'s truck and took off, first to see the cattle on J.B.'s ranch and then to see the construction site of what's now our headquarters in Lowell.

"He took us down into what was to be the computer room," John recalled. "He said, 'Right here in this room, every truckload transaction that takes place in America will be processed by our computers.' He was saying they were going to be the truckload broker for the whole industry. That never totally took place, but certainly the asset-light truck brokerage concept has gotten to be a fairly big operation. And they're not done growing that part of the business."

That part of the business is not just ICS, which is our brokerage segment. It now includes an emerging part of our organization that, frankly, represents a distinctively purple future—technology innovations.

For much of JBHT's history, technology played what you'd probably call a "supportive" role in the business. That changed dramatically in 2016 when Stuart Scott joined our team as executive vice president and chief information officer. Stuart replaced Kay Lewis, who retired after twenty-seven years of service. Kay had been the perfect person for the job during her tenure, and Stuart was the perfect person to take her place as we transitioned into a new approach to technology.

Stuart grew up in Kentucky in a blue-collar family that valued hard work and integrity, but didn't encourage higher education. "My dad was an awesome person and he gave me a lot of great character advice," Stuart told us, "but he wasn't much for the white-collar environment." Stuart was on his own when he left home after high school, but he had great grades and a desire to pursue something different. He worked his way through the University of Louisville, earning undergraduate and master's degrees in computer engineering, and then he earned an MBA at Vanderbilt. That set him up for a career in engineering and IT that saw him work his way through several opportunities with GE businesses, including a stint with GE Healthcare in London. He also worked for Microsoft, TB&W, and Tempur-Sealy.

Early in his career, someone told Stuart he was an "architect and a builder" and not a "landlord." He didn't appreciate it much at the time, he said, but it proved prophetic.

"He was right," Stuart said. "I'm not the type of person who keeps the status quo."

That made him a perfect fit for J.B. Hunt Transport.

"I was looking for a company that was in the process or really committed to going through a transformation and dramatic change," he said. "J.B. Hunt was certainly in that phase. Of course, every company says they want to be digital and transformational and all of those buzzwords. But there were characteristics at J.B. Hunt that I really felt were meaningful, characteristics that said that they were serious about it."

Stuart recognized that we had a culture of entrepreneurship, even if in some ways it had been a bit dormant for a few years while we focused on operational excellence.

"It was still there," he said. "It just needed to be fueled and reignited."

And, in fact, our focus on operational excellence had led to another characteristic that attracted Stuart to our team. He saw a stable, healthy company that was well positioned to commit the resources required to stretch itself in a transformative way. He saw a company that had big ideas, the resources to fund those ideas, the leadership to do it the right way, and the willingness to commit to it. And he saw a company that was investing in technology for the right reasons—because it was good for the customer.

The proof came in April 2017 when we announced a five-year $500 million investment into technology innovation—$136 million to enhance our operating system, $141 million to modernize our infrastructure, and $223 million to create innovative and disruptive technology.

"That caught people's attention in the industry more than I thought," said Stuart. "I felt like that's the kind of investment everybody's making, but clearly not."

The end-game, as Stuart sees it, is to transform JBHT from an "asset company with technology into a technology company with assets." What that looks like is subject to changes in the market—to customer needs and demands, to advancements in technology, and to the decisions made by our competition.

"What we've tried to do is create a regular cadence on taking external information—what our competitors are doing, where venture capital money is going, partnerships that are forming, acquisitions, and those types of things—and seeing how they influence our path," he said. "But it doesn't necessarily change the end-game."

Interestingly, many of our traditional asset-based competitors are not our biggest concern when it comes to technology innovation. Some aren't financially healthy enough to invest the way we're investing. And some simply are not willing to take the risks. Even some of our brokerage competitors who are asset-light have, to date, seemed fairly content to roll with their current business models and offerings. Start-ups, on the other hand, don't have ties to existing infrastructure and they aren't held captive by legacy processes or systems. And many of them have ample financial backing from venture capitalists.

One of our biggest initiatives has been to provide "visibility" into where freight is at any given time. We weren't pushed in that direction by our traditional competitors. We moved in that direction because our customers needed it. Software-based companies like Fourkites, Tenfour, and Macropoint were filling that need, but we weren't and neither was anyone else in the transportation services industry. Even Fourth Party Logistics companies (4PLs) weren't giving their customers visibility to where their freight is at any point in time.

"I was shocked that a company whose business is to provide a holistic solution for a shipper, such as a 4PL, wouldn't make technology inherently part of the value equation of outsourcing," Stuart said. "That told me two things. One, there's a lot of opportunity to do things that aren't necessarily new or innovative but that are advanced for this industry. And, two, that if we don't do it and customers really want it, they're going to go buy it from someone else. If they're buying technology from somebody else, that means that technology company has more data and information about our customer than we do. That's not acceptable. I don't like any company to come between me and my customer."

Stuart has seen venture capital firms placing multiple bets on complementary start-ups that, if combined, would create solutions competitive to what we offer. Those software companies that are providing visibility into freight location, for example, are gathering data that might position them, on their own or by combining with other companies, to move into the 4PL space. Our goal is to build a team that is on equal footing or ahead of such would-be competitors. To do that, JBHT must view technology through a different lens. When he first arrived, Stuart asked his team how they envisioned the scale of their work, and the responses centered on supporting JBHT's fleet.

"You're not thinking about this thing the right way," he told them. "We're building a platform for a trillion-dollar industry. JBHT employees just happen to be early adopters of that technology. We're going to take everything we do and turn it inside out. We're going to start externally on building our technology strategy and then work inward. We're going to build for customer first."

That was very different from using technology to back-end support an asset business.

"One of the strategic pillars that I talk about is that we don't build technology for our 22,000 employees," Stuart said. "We build technology for the 3.5 million drivers and the millions of shippers who are out there. Our employees are included in that equation as a critical user base. But we have to put our technology in the hands of our customers and suppliers and everyone we do business with. That's going to be the differentiator. And the fact we have assets puts us in an enviable position against any start-up out there. The shippers need to know their stuff is going to be picked up and it's going to arrive where it needs to arrive. Their business and their job depend on that. They need someone they can rely on. A technology-only company is not a reliable source. Shippers aren't going to leave it to chance. Our assets are a differentiator. Our technology needs to be a differentiator, too."

Upside Down

Two things are happening that Stuart believes will "completely turn everything upside down" in the transportation services industry. First, nearly every adult in America holds technology, literally, in the palm of their hands. A Pew

Research Center survey conducted in 2018 found that 77 percent of Americans own a smartphone, up from 35 percent in 2011 when the center first began surveying on that topic. The trend is growing within every age group and economic class. For instance, 73 percent of adults ages fifty to sixty-four own a smartphone, as does 67 percent of households earning less than $30,000 a year.[1]

Gartner, the technology research and advisory firm, estimates that 20 billion devices will be connected to the Internet by 2020—giving them all real-time access to information about everything from their location to the weather forecast and from traffic conditions to fuel prices.

"Now you have technology in the hands of a critical part of the supply-demand equation," Stuart said.

The second factor is the ability to track freight and provide visibility to its location. The cost of equipping trucks and trailers with location devices has decreased dramatically in recent years, and we've reached the point where nearly everything moving can have a beacon that transmits data about its location. That's why a big part of the $141 million we're investing to modernize our infrastructure is going toward enhancements to our fleet that make it more efficient, safer, and better connected to each other, to us, and to shippers.

"So, the data is there and the tool is there and in the hands of the users," Stuart says. "And with software and Artificial Intelligence (AI), we're now able to turn that into value."

We're now able to monitor supply chain conditions for our business partners and customers in real time, which improves efficiencies, communication, service, and overall performance through each phase of a product's shipment. When circumstances change, we can respond quickly, nimbly, and with confidence.

This is creating changes to the JBHT business model that are unique and help us stand out from the competitors in our field. For instance, we've more than doubled our software team and we're developing software products and applications that anyone can buy and use, some of which we might give away.

One example is our Transportation Management System (TMS) that does things no commercial TMS can do. It provides dynamic mode selection by day, by mode, and by package. And it can make two million routing decisions

---

1. "Mobile Fact Sheet," Pew Research Center, February 5, 2018, available at http://www.pewinternet.org/fact-sheet/mobile, accessed April 23, 2018.

a minute. In other industries, such as manufacturing, a TMS is not where you invest your money and create intellectual property, but it's an obvious place for us to invest and it's always been an amazing but proprietary tool in our competitive toolshed.

"We have arguably the best Transportation Management System in the world," Stuart said, "but we keep it all to ourselves. That's gonna change."

Providing technology to shippers and carriers solves their problems and, in the process, draws them to us as their partner of choice. It's innovative and disruptive, but that's the way we stay purple on the inside.

"Our competitors in many ways are really software companies like Oracle and SAP," Stuart said. "I say that not because I want to just sell software. I'm not interested in just selling a license to use our TMS system. I want a deeper relationship. Technology may be where that starts. But if we use technology to pull them in, our customer focus and operational excellence will make us a bigger part of their supply chain."

Transporting e-Commerce

The most visible example of how this is coming to life is with J.B. Hunt 360, our cloud-based e-commerce product platform that serves shippers and carriers. It includes four main components that work together to give us a competitive advantage.

The "Connector" allows users to interact with us any way they want—manually, over the web, with mobile devices, Electronic Data Interchange (EDI), Applications Programming Interface (APIs), blockchain technology. . . . Whatever technology, whatever data communication methods are used, it provides access to all of our engineering intellectual property—our algorithms, our artificial intelligence, our things that make very smart decisions in real time based on enormous amounts of data.

This ensures we're feeding the right information into the 360 Marketplace, which is our transactional system. Jobs are priced and scoped correctly and advanced leads are fed to the right carriers who are most interested in that freight through load recommendations. It helps optimize less-than-truckload options and makes parcel and mode selections based on service levels.

"Not a lot of companies have around a hundred engineers who do nothing but build optimization algorithms and AI," Stuart said.

The 360 Marketplace is where shippers and carriers access products like our Transportation Management System or our warehouse management software. It's where we use data to match shippers with carriers who can best meet the shipper's needs. Shortly after launching 360 Marketplace, we were averaging about a hundred accepted offers a week. That means there were no phone calls, just clicks. Thousands of carriers and shippers already are using the system. By midway through 2018, we were averaging more than 7,000 accepted offers a week and breaking our records for acceptances, loads, searches, revenue, and/or margin a couple of times each month.

The last piece is the management console that provides visibility so shippers can see everything that's going on in their entire supply chain. It includes all of the dials and the levers and predictive analytics so they can take preventative and predictive actions that make everything run smoother and more efficiently.

"We're 60-plus percent asset utilization in this industry," Stuart said. "That's crazy. With the costs of our assets, it should be well north of that. This technology is how we improve that dramatically."

A Culture of Tech

One of the marks of a company that's purple on the inside is that it knows its identity, stays true to its identity, and yet isn't controlled or confined by its identity. Innovation requires disruption, and an organization that's become a slave to its past will never reinvent its future. Our investment in technology provides a case in point.

You might recall that JBHT has such a strong culture that, as I put it previously, it tends to reject organ transplants. In other words, we haven't always done well with acquisitions or with hiring leaders from outside our own walls. So, what did we do when we decided to invest more heavily in technology innovation? We hired from the outside and less than two years later we made a significant acquisition.

Stuart is the only top-level executive in the company who hadn't spent at least twenty years with JBHT, so he doesn't have the benefit of growing up in our culture. On the other hand, he doesn't have the blinders that sometimes block the vision of those of us who are thoroughly soaked in the JBHT ways.

"You can only be so innovative inside your own four walls," John Roberts points out. "We knew we had to go outside. With the acceleration of thinking of people from other parts of the world who come here to an open culture with an open mind and the power of the foundation of our culture, we're going to meet the times. We may not beat them but we're going to meet them. It's going fast right now."

Our past difficulties with leaders from the outside wasn't a roadblock, but it was a valuable lesson that guided how we've moved forward in technology. Stuart was a great hire not just because he brought an outside perspective and a disruptive mindset, but because his blue-collar background blends in perfectly at J.B. Hunt Transport.

"I grew up that way," he said. "I felt very comfortable that the people here really value work and rolling up your sleeves and doing what you have to do to do the best thing for the customer. They had not hired an outside executive in twenty-three years, so, basically, never. But I knew what I was getting into. And coming in and meeting with the leadership and getting an understanding of the culture and history of the company, it felt like a good fit."

Stuart provided us with a change agent, not a nuclear option for our technology organization. He arrived with a respect for our business and the people who've brought us where we are, so he didn't clean house, he just built something unique on top of our foundation. He's grown the team, not replaced the team. The newcomers have provided a fresh perspective and new skills, while the holdovers have provided company and industry insights to go with a renewed passion for their work.

"You don't have to replace a lot of people," Stuart said. "You bring in a few catalysts and role models, and it inspires other people. A technology person's value to the company and shareholders is not that they know a particular technology as much as it's that they know the business and they know how technology applies to the business. There are great people in the technology organization, and they can contribute in significant ways. Many times, it's about supporting them and putting them in a position to be successful by giving them a vision and strategy and purpose to what they do. Give them a strong vision and they get excited. We chose this career because we want to build software. It vibrates beyond our employees and into the community. People can feel that it's a different company."

As previously explained, Stuart has helped create a new version of our technology segment, one that sees its role as more of a software company than of a support system. That's been an exciting and invigorating change for his team, but harder at times for the nontechnology parts of the business. They've had to learn that building technology is difficult. By definition, Stuart says, building software is new every time. It's a bit like running a manufacturing facility where every day you try to produce a new product that's different than yesterday's.

To their credit, the rest of our leadership team has embraced the value of technology investments as a means for meeting our business needs. That's why we were among the first companies to place an order reserving electric tractors from Tesla. We'll start by using these energy-efficient trucks in our West Coast DCS operations, primarily on local and dray routes. And that's why we were open to acquiring Special Logistics Dedicated, a Houston-based distribution company that will enhance our ability to expand our e-commerce and final mile delivery, especially when it comes to "big and bulky" items.

The entrepreneurship fueled and reignited by our technology transformation provided some inertia to investigate options for such an acquisition, but we moved forward because it was a right fit for our business needs. We have created a strategy for building an end-to-end supply chain solution for our customers—first mile, middle mile, and final mile. With that strategy in mind, the discussion shifts to how we get there. Do we build what we lack or buy it? SLD provided an extension of what we already do and helped meet some strategic needs for our vision.

"This company is not afraid to repeat history in a positive sense," Stuart said. "But we have to prove success. Early indications are good, but we'll see. Time will tell."

Investments in technology innovation, whether it's in the $500 million commitment to upgrades and disruptions or in a $136 million acquisition of another company, might seem like risks, but they're essential to the health of a purple cow.

"You get yourself in big trouble if you don't invest," John said. "The most dangerous thing we can do is to not pay attention to changing times, today more than ever."

CHAPTER 11

Standing Still = Falling Behind

If what you did yesterday seems big, you haven't done anything today.
— Lou Holtz, former football coach

J.B. Hunt Transport became purple on the inside because of its people. That's what every company really is—a collection of people. Our people, whether they work in cabs, terminals, warehouses, or the corporate offices, have developed and lived the innovative, disruptive personality that makes us different and creates our success. It only makes sense, then, that our future rests in our ability to recruit, develop, and retain leaders who understand how we got where we are and who can take the company new places we never imagined.

In the early years of the company's growth, leaders emerged somewhat organically out of the sales or operations teams. We expanded mainly by adding new terminals that stretched our reach to new parts of the country. And because we were still small, it wasn't hard to spot the leaders who were ready to advance. It was sort of the "best athlete" model where the coaches look around at the available talent and then give the ball to the person with the best skills to move it down the field. When we would open a new terminal, we would look around to see which salesman or operations manager could best advance the ball. We looked for people with great financial statistics and who had demonstrated natural leadership skills, great rapport with people (especially with drivers), and a bias for action and for creating solutions.

Mark Greenway, who joined JBHT's manager trainee program in 1987 and now is senior vice president of human relations, points out that our early, informal approach to succession planning, "rewarded the action-oriented person more than the introspective, thoughtful person. It was a culture for a long time that emphasized staying busy and getting a lot done." Things began to shift in the mid-1990s, thanks in large part to advancements in technology and software that allowed us to more accurately track effectiveness as well as efficiency.

"We became more thoughtful in the ways we evaluated people," Mark told us. "We became much more of a spreadsheet culture and an analytical culture."

We still looked for the same leadership attributes, but it became increasingly important, especially as the numbers got bigger, that leaders had a deeper understanding of those numbers and the levers that caused them to move. Still, most business units did their own succession planning until the early 2000s when, as Mark puts it, "we started thinking about succession planning as an HR practice rather than just a business necessity."

Many of our leaders have emerged from our college recruiting program, but that program, and our management training program that it feeds, have changed over the years. The original management training program was pretty generic. The trainees spent a month in each department, then moved into whatever role was deemed best for them and the company. Now each segment has a ninety-day program designed specifically for its leaders.

We once put a priority on recruiting only from the universities with the top transportation and supply chain programs—Penn State, Ohio State, the University of Tennessee, Iowa State, and, of course, the nearby Sam Walton College of Business at the University of Arkansas. We didn't always get the top draft choices, so to speak, but we'd usually land three or four of the top eight. Some worked out great and remain with us today. Some, however, didn't stay around long. When we were primarily a truckload company, we couldn't promote them fast enough, so we lost a few really good leaders who started their own companies or went to work for other companies. Others left because they weren't a good fit for what is a tough job. Our managers don't start out with a mahogany desk. They typically begin their careers in a loud environment working with a blue-collar workforce. That's not for everyone.

We didn't abandon the top-tier university graduates, but, as Mark put it, "We pivoted a little and focused more on the military and blue-collar kids." We expanded our recruiting to include more secondary schools, where we found students who had worked their way through college and were part of up-and-coming supply chain programs. Or we found veterans who had leadership experience in the military and were used to working odd hours in challenging environments.

"Putting you in a warehouse in east New Jersey is a lot better work environment than being shot at somewhere," Mark said. "The pay's better and the environment's better than what they had."

Meanwhile, with the growth of our purple cow segments, we began to need more leaders in our pipeline. So, in the early 2000s, our succession planning became more formal and involved more forecasting. We could look at our growth rates and forecast how many director-level leaders we would need, and then recruit the right number of college students and veterans to meet that need down the road.

Now we have a six-year path through our leadership pipeline. In DCS alone, we've gone from thirteen trainees a year to more than two hundred. After a ninety-day training program, they are assigned as a manager somewhere around the country. After about two years, most advance to an account manager role, where they are responsible for the profit and loss of a small to large fleet, and then to regional operations manager, which makes them eligible for stock options. Along the way, they go through Leadership 101 training, which covers basic leadership skills and JBHT culture. In Leadership 201, they learn technical skills like how to use our software programs and how to execute our standard operating procedures (SOPs). Then they go through Leadership 301, which focuses on strategic leadership and produces the candidates for regional operations managers.

Top-down, Bottom-up

Those leaders, however, aren't locked into a career in DCS. We take a top-down, bottom-up approach to career development that allows our leadership pipeline to feed every segment of the company.

It begins with our HR team meeting with entry-level managers annually to help assess their career objectives so we can connect them with opportunities throughout the organization, not just in the area where they are working. One of Mark's primary battles is to fight the popular idea among younger leaders that they need to change jobs every three or four years so they can experience something new and different. He wants them to realize they can continually reinvent themselves within JBHT.

Here's how he typically makes his case: "When I started with the company, we were about $250,000 million in revenue," he said. "Today we're about

$7 billion. If you look at the growth plans for the next ten years, we'll easily double that. If you look at twenty years, we'll triple where we are today. That means employees today will have twice the opportunity in the next ten to twenty years as I had in the last thirty. There's no reason for you to go anywhere else. The opportunity exists at J.B. Hunt. I just need to help you find it. We're going to grow, and we need these skill sets. If you want a career, we've got a place for you. That new job exists at J.B. Hunt. It's in Intermodal vs. ICS or ICS vs. Truck. Or you can go from engineering to IT. You don't have to stay on some narrow path."

That's the grassroots piece. The top-down part involves HR going to the company's leaders—from the board of directors down to the director level—and asking them for the names of two or three people they have in mind as their successor. Mark and his team use tools like Workday, an advanced HR software, to track readiness of emerging leaders. Then they bring the top-down and bottom-up practices together so that high potential leaders aren't overlooked.

"We've worked to dispel that feeling that advancement is about 'who you know' and show folks that there's a methodology and science behind it," he said. "For instance, we have calibration sessions where we bring managers in and we nine-box based on potential and performance. We'll take an entire level of senior managers and plot them on the nine-box grid. We have very intentional conversations to ensure they are rated appropriately. Those in the upper right box are the highest performance and potential and should be promoted next. Then the question is where should they go? Do they need to stay in their business unit, or do they need some other type of experience?"

This creates well-vetted talent pools from which we can draw on as we discuss openings and potential openings across the organization.

"When you ask leaders who their three people are who might replace them, they naturally think about the people who report to them," Mark said. "We'll bring this talent pool up and ask, 'Could some of these folks potentially come in and be your successor or be part of your team?'"

Having a deep understanding of the existing talent pools also allows us to know when we need to look outside the company, as was the case when we shifted our approach toward technology and engineering.

"Growing organically is really healthy and really great for your culture, but you do have to inject outside thinking strategically and purposefully from time to time," Mark says. "It's like a Vitamin B shot that gives you a boost."

Succession planning—the way we recruit, develop, and advance our leaders—is essential to our future. We need bright, innovative leaders who are committed to JBHT's values and hungry to build on our purple cow history.

Creatively Dissatisfied

Entrepreneurship. Innovation. Disruption.

Can they co-exist with execution? Stability? Consistency?

Indeed, they can. And they must.

Purple cows die of starvation if they aren't fed on the fruits of execution, but execution without a unique and compelling vision is both boring and fattening. Who wants to chew that cud?

If you've gotten nothing else from the story of JBHT, hopefully you've learned that standing still equals falling behind. Standing still can feel comfortable and safe, and, yes, there are times to pause and reflect before moving in one direction or another. But hesitate too long, and you're lost. Wait too long, and the competition will pass you by. That's the fate of ordinary cows.

When I would try to convince investors or would-be investors that JBHT was a good stock play, I often focused on the enduring nature of the freight transportation industry. "You can live without frozen yogurt," I would say, "but a thriving economy cannot survive without transportation." That's still true, and it bodes well for JBHT's future. But the freight transportation industry doesn't look the same as it did in the 1970s when we entered the trucking business . . . or as it did in the 1980s when we went public . . . or as it did in the 1990s when we launched Intermodal . . . or as it does today.

Companies that are purple on the inside understand what it means to be creatively dissatisfied. If you get comfortable, fat, and happy, then rest assured that you're on the precipice of decline. The creatively dissatisfied aren't unhappy; they simply have an unending desire to improve. They don't stand still. They move with a purpose. They are purple to the core.

That's how we see J.B. Hunt Transport—purple to the core.

In June 2017, John Roberts gave a presentation to Wall Street that I think revealed our inner nature, because it reflected our commitment to both disruption and execution. He talked through our strategic plan to "achieve $10 billion in quality revenue" by 2020. And he told them "we are prepared to elevate and disrupt supply chain management across North America by bringing innovative solutions, enabled by cutting-edge technology, to our customers' fingertips."

In an internal email to our team about the presentation, John echoed the words of another CEO in our region, who shares the commitment to "compete with technology" but "win with people." He praised our people for their part in past successes, and he made it clear that our future rests in their ability to execute going forward. And here's how he signed off in that email: "Are you with us? #disrupt."

Look closely at those messages, and you'll notice that being purple on the inside isn't a license to act irresponsibly. In fact, John, along with CFO Dave Mee, have a shared commitment to one simple but powerful rule of thumb that at first glance might seem counter to that call for disruption: You gotta make a quality return on invested capital.

"Don't ask us for any money if you don't have a compelling return," John said. "Don't even bother. It's gotta be solid on plan, time, and measurement. You've gotta have a return and you have to maintain a return."

That's the difference between a wild idea and an idea that separates you from the competition. One is backed by insights and planning and driven by a commitment to execution. The other is just fantasy.

Founders often worry more about the size of the company than the quality of returns, and our company went through that stage. But long-term success isn't tied to size as much as quality. As John puts it, "We just want to make a lot of really good, quality money." So, we've pushed forward with a dual focus on innovation that's driven by disruption but founded on execution. Growth is a likely byproduct, but it has to be based on a quality return.

"That has really been a guiding light for us," John said.

That guiding light, if we follow it, will keep us purple on the inside while leading us into a long and strong future.

JBHT, like all corporations, should see itself like a product with no expiration date on its relevance. We should think and act as though we will always be in business, but we have to work hard and disrupt at times to make that vision a reality. Past successes do not guarantee future success. It takes creativity, the best people, a clear and communicable strategy, services that provide outstanding solutions to customer needs, vision, and, most of all, execution for any business to maintain its place at or near the top of the market.

We celebrate the victories of the past. We cherish the lessons learned from good times and bad times because they help us shape the future. We are thankful for the contributions of those no longer in the huddle. But we must invest heavily in terms of time, talent, and resources to ensure JBHT exceeds the accomplishments of the past and surpasses our greatest expectations for the future.